The Pastoral Counselor in Social Action

Speed Leas
Paul Kittlaus

Fortress Press   Philadelphia

Creative Pastoral Care and Counseling Series
  Editor: Howard J. Clinebell
  Associate Editor: Howard W. Stone
The Care and Counseling of Youth in the Church by Paul B. Irwin
*Growth Counseling for Marriage Enrichment: Pre-Marriage and the
  Early Years* by Howard J. Clinebell
Crisis Counseling by Howard W. Stone
Pastoral Care and Counseling in Grief and Separation
  by Wayne E. Oates
Counseling for Liberation by Charlotte Holt Clinebell
Growth Counseling for Mid-Years Couples by Howard J. Clinebell
Theology and Pastoral Care by John B. Cobb, Jr.
Pastor and Parish—A Systems Approach by E. Mansell Pattison
Pastoral Care with Handicapped Persons by Lowell G. Colston
Care and Counseling of the Aging by William M. Clements
Anger and Assertiveness in Pastoral Care by David W. Augsburger
Using Behavioral Methods in Pastoral Counseling
  by Howard W. Stone
New Approaches to Family Pastoral Care by Douglas A. Anderson
The Pastoral Counselor in Social Action
  by Speed Leas and Paul Kittlaus

To Our Children
Jocelyn, Mark, Winston, Adam,
Ellen, Ann, Nathaniel,
and Glenn

Library of Congress Cataloging in Publication Data
Leas, Speed, 1937–
    The pastoral counselor in social action.
    (Creative pastoral care and counseling series)
    Bibliography: p.
    1. Pastoral counseling.   2. Social action.
  I. Kittlaus, Paul, 1934–   joint author. II. Title.
    BV4012.L39   253   80–8059
    ISBN 0–8006–0565–9

8281G80   Printed in the United States of America   1–565

Contents

Series Foreword

Let me share with you some of the hopes that are in the minds of those of us who helped to develop this series—hopes that relate directly to you as the reader. It is our desire and expectation that these books will be of help to you in developing better working tools as a minister counselor. We hope that they will do this by encouraging your own creativity in developing more effective methods and programs for helping people live life more fully. It is our intention in this series to affirm the many things you have going for you as a minister in helping troubled persons—the many assets and resources from your religious heritage, your role as the leader of a congregation, and your unique relationship to individuals and families throughout the life cycle. We hope to help you reaffirm the *power of the pastoral* by the use of fresh models and methods in your ministry.

The aim of the series is not to be comprehensive with respect to topics but rather to bring innovative approaches to some major types of counseling. Although the books are practice-oriented, they also provide a solid foundation of theological and psychological insights. They are written primarily for ministers (and those preparing for the ministry) but we hope that they will also prove useful to other counselors who are interested in the crucial role of spiritual and value issues in all helping relationships. In addition we hope that the series will be useful in seminary courses, clergy support groups, continuing education workshops, and lay befriender training.

This is a period of rich new developments in counseling and

psychotherapy. The time is ripe for a flowering of creative methods and insights in pastoral care and counseling. Our expectation is that this series will stimulate grass roots creativity as innovative methods and programs come alive for you. Some of the major thrusts that will be discussed in this series include a new awareness of the unique contributions of the theologically trained counselor, the liberating power of the human potentials orientation, an appreciation of the pastoral care function of the ministering congregation, the importance of humanizing systems and institutions as well as close relationships, the importance of pastoral *care* (and not just counseling), the many opportunities for caring ministries throughout the life cycle, the deep changes in male-female relationships, and the new psychotherapies such as Gestalt therapy, Transactional Analysis, educative counseling, and crisis methods. Our hope is that this series will enhance your resources for your ministry to persons by opening doorways to understanding of these creative thrusts in pastoral care and counseling.

This volume addresses one of the most crucial and perplexing problems in the practice of ministry—how to integrate the healing and care of individuals with healing and care of those societal structures which diminish individual wholeness so profoundly. As most pastors know from experience, it is difficult to keep a chasm from developing between the pastoral-priestly and the prophetic dimensions of one's ministry. The polarizing within a congregation between those who are committed exclusively to personal caring and those who are interested only in social change is equally hard to avoid. Yet, if a congregation is to become a center for fostering whole-persons-in-a-wholeness-nurturing-society, it is essential that these two aspects of ministry work together in complementary ways. To be such a center is the clear call of the biblical vision of the church in the context of today's oppression-torn global village. The privatizing of pastoral care and counseling is a constant and seductive temptation in ministry. So is the process which leads to the alienation of social action from pastoral care. The pressing needs of the world today makes the bringing together of these two vital dimensions of ministry increasingly important.

In this book, Speed Leas and Paul Kittlaus bring to bear on this fundamental pastoral problem the wisdom acquired during years of rich experiences in social change ministries. Their twin motifs are that holistic pastoral care must include care and healing of institutional structures (not just of individuals and intimate relationships) and that effective social action must incorporate pastoral care awareness and skills. (The companion truth which is not emphasized in this book is that helping people become empowered as community change agents is often an essential ingredient in their personal healing and growth.) After describing the importance of defining pastoral care holistically, they describe practical ways to increase the effectiveness and person-enhancingness of social action by using a wide variety of personal care and relationship-building methods.

The authors distinguish five categories of parishioners—those whose painful personal problems make it impossible for them to become involved in societal concerns; those who are feeling some pain from social injustices and therefore can be enlisted in social change ministries; those already involved but needing further support and training to increase their effectiveness; those desiring to do more; and those who are not yet ready to get involved because of their inner resistances. The authors chose not to deal with the first category since the other volumes in this series focus mainly on the healing and growth needs of such persons. But they describe in detail how to work in caring, empowering ways with persons in the other four categories. They show how to use pastoral care approaches in identifying and training an action group, how to develop and implement an action plan, and how to overcome the blocks to social change action.

I first got to know Speed and Paul and to appreciate their expertise in social action in the sixties when they were codirectors of the ecumenical Center for Metropolitan Mission In-Service Training in Los Angeles. Speed now lives in Michigan. He is a consultant to church leaders (both ordained and lay) and to denominational executives on issues such as organizational development, conflict management, community analysis, social change ministries, and clergy development. Paul is director of the national Office of Church and Society of the United Church of

Christ in Washington, D.C. He has specific responsibilities for
health and welfare, economic justice, and food policy issues. My
perception of Speed and Paul is that each brings the two thrusts
of this volume together in his own style of ministry, integrating
pastoral care skills and sensitivities with social action training
and practice.

I predict that this book will prove to be a valuable guide for
pastors and for laypersons who want to become more effective in
helping to heal the tragic malignancies of our society—racism,
sexism, economic injustice, ageism, and social oppression. These
malignancies in the body of our society cripple and diminish full
personhood on a massive, wholesale scale while we counselors,
therapists, and teachers seek to repair the damage on an individualistic, retail basis. A viable strategy for ministry today obviously must include and integrate both personal care and social
change. I expect that this book will also prove useful for those
in nonchurch settings who desire to increase the effectiveness of
their social action by adding personal care approaches.

Believing passionately in the critical importance of the main
thrust of this book, I commend it to you, the reader, with the
hope and expectation that it will become a significant resource
in your practice of the kind of holistic pastoral care which our
broken, bleeding planet so desperately needs.

HOWARD J. CLINEBELL

Preface

Rolf and Marie Harden sent their son to public school expecting that the teachers, administrators, and students there would be involved with each other in ways that might assure Bud of healthy and enjoyable learning and growth experiences. They expected that he would learn the requisite academic skills, learn how to get along with other children, learn certain values regarding the worth and integrity of persons, and that he would find these learning experiences to be rich, exciting, and rewarding. Instead, the boy came home day after day despondent and defeated. As the weeks passed, he became more withdrawn and quiet. The first report card revealed poor grades and his teacher wrote several remarks on the card about Bud's bad manners and disruptive behavior in the classroom.

The parents came to their pastor, Alice Markel, for help. An experienced counselor, the Reverend Alice Markel wanted first of all to investigate the various possible causes of the problem. Could it be that Bud has a learning defect? Is the teaching itself inferior? Are the other children hostile and cruel? Is the school in need of better tools or books? The source of the difficulty could conceivably have been located in any of these—or other— areas of concern. The pastor wanted to give full consideration to a wide and complex variety of factors. Some of these factors may indeed have been regarded as "Bud's problem," factors involving attitude and motivation or learning abilities. Other factors, however, may have been inherent in the system itself, the personnel, or the school climate, policies, or teaching equipment and resources.

Pastor Markel would have been less than helpful had she assumed that Bud's difficulties stemmed entirely from his own personal inadequacy—*if* in fact the problem derived mainly from, for example, poor supervision in the classroom and playground. To limit her help under such circumstances to counseling for the individual child would have been to invest her energy, and that of the family, in an enterprise that could hardly have improved the situation. Her efforts would have been equally unhelpful, however, were she to have proceeded on the opposite assumption: that Bud Harden did *not* need her help and support.

What the pastor did was to encourage the parents to investigate fully all possible sources of the difficulty within the school itself. She helped the Hardens communicate with their son about his understanding of the problems at school. She encouraged them to talk with other parents, and with other children in Bud's class, as well as with the teacher, the principal, and other personnel at the school. This made it possible for the parents to identify a variety of possible problem sources within the school—as well as within the child—that might have led to his poor performance and dissatisfaction.

Much of the literature in pastoral care has focused on ministering to the needs of individual church members and their families. This book is directed toward ministries which change the environment in which such individuals live. We will be concerned here with the support systems that affect the lives of people.

Because the Hardens were able to look not only at their child but also at the environment in which he was expected to learn, they had a fuller range of tools with which to cope with the difficulties they were facing. Pastor Markel of course invited the Hardens to look closely at their family life, but she also sent them out to discover how the school environment was affecting their child's learning as well. After talking with teachers, other parents, and the school administration, the Hardens were convinced that if there was any one reason why Bud was having trouble in school it was probably that the student-teacher ratio was too high for the teachers to be able to maintain discipline in the classroom. The teachers needed help both inside the school and on the playground. They simply had too many students to be able to manage their groups and create an effective and humane learning environment. Using the techniques to be described in this book, Pastor Markel and the Hardens called together a number of people who both had children in the same school and were members of the same congregation. Together they formed a group to study and address the problems at Bud's school.

This book seeks to help pastors use both counseling skills and social action skills. Because other books in the Creative Pastoral Care and Counseling Series focus more heavily on the counseling side of a full ministry of pastoral care, we will here stress the social action side. Readers will be helped to identify persons who can potentially become partners in social action ministries, and will be given ideas and plans potentially useful in forming and guiding healthy and effective social action groups.

This approach assumes that God demands obedience and calls us to minister to individuals, groups, and systems. We assume that in a ministry of pastoral care we are not called to make of others "the enemy" (as has been the case in some approaches to social action), nor are we called only to be active listeners, perhaps helping people adjust to conditions that may in themselves be evil (as has been the case in some approaches to counseling). We assume that the task of pastoral care is to help individuals, groups, and systems reestablish their broken relationships to each other and to God. In all of this we believe that no person or group is beyond God's grace, none is beyond our care, and there is always hope for positive change.

We wish to acknowledge the help and assistance that we have received from a number of persons in the writing of this manuscript. Thanks are due especially to Howard Clinebell and Howard Stone, the editors of this series. Their unlimited patience and supportive critique have been greatly appreciated. Geraldine Harper, Robert McKay, and Janet Vandevender have contributed immeasurably in connection with the revising of the manuscript. We are also grateful to Marilyn Cook and Carol Cunningham for their careful typing at various stages in the project.

1. Pastoral Counseling and Social Action

During the 1960s one of the authors of this book was addressing a convention of Clinical Pastoral Educators when a member of the audience yelled, "All you Social Action guys are operating out of unresolved personalities!" Across the auditorium a counter-charge was immediately voiced: "You Clinical Pastoral Educators are part of the pacification program." Such mutual accusations and rebuttal have characterized the contention between pastoral counselors and social actionists over the past twenty years.

Contention in Pastoral Care

Many of the arguments in the controversy have merit and should be looked at as possible sources for fresh understanding. Each ministerial focus, particularly when operating in isolation, can become a caricature of what it was originally intended to be. Balanced criticism, therefore, can perhaps help the reader identify some of the deficiencies that arise where ministry is practiced exclusively within one area of competence.

Pastoral Counseling

In the late forties and early fifties one aspect of pastoral care came into its own as a distinct discipline, one that altered the theoretical foundation of ministry. That discipline was pastoral counseling. The new technologies of the counseling movement influenced not only the practice of ministry, but also the ways in which Christians think about such theological issues as sin and forgiveness. Seminaries changed their curricula to include courses on counseling. The Clinical Pastoral Education movement blossomed. And clergy accommodated their one-on-one professional relationships and even their preaching to the methods and values of the emerging counseling movement.

The seminal ideas of this ministerial speciality were provided by Carl Rogers, Seward Hiltner, David Roberts, Wayne Oates, and Carroll Wise.* Under the impetus of these mentors and the institutions spawned by their writings there developed a pastoral emphasis on counseling as a distinct enterprise.

This counseling ministry was marked by certain characteristic features. It was (1) directed to the individual; (2) focused on personal motivation; (3) concerned about trust, care, and support to create an environment in which change will take place; (4) concerned about relationships; and (5) included such change targets as: changing an unhealthy marriage, making a vocational choice, coping with physical illness, and dealing with grief and separation.

Social Action

In the sixties a different ministerial function, social action, acquired a life and vigor that it had not enjoyed since before World War II. It certainly did not eclipse the counseling movement but in a new sphere paralleled the technologies directed toward the care of individual souls.

The civil rights movement was perhaps the single most influential event in calling the professional ministry to social action. As clergy became involved in actions directed toward the desegregation of schools, the integration of lunch counters in the South, the elimination of de facto residential segregation in the North, and the implementation of voting rights for minorities, new institutions and ideologies began to appear in the church to undergird these ministries.

Key writings of this era included the books of Saul Alinsky, Gibson Winter, and Harvey Cox, as well as those by George Younger, George Webber, Colin Williams, and the collection of papers prepared by the United States Conference for the World Council of Churches Department of Studies in Evangelism entitled *Planning for Mission.** Institutions grew up for the purpose of training and encouraging these social action ministries. Among them were the East Harlem Protestant Parish, numerous action training centers, the Delta Ministry, Clergy and Laity Concerned, and many other organizations (usually ecumenical) directed at social change.

This movement developed a pastoral emphasis on social action that again had its special characteristics. It was (1) directed toward the policies or practices of organizations; (2) focused on forces in the environment that shape behavior; (3) concerned about power, influence, rewards, and punishments to create an environment in which change could take place; (4) concerned about issues; and (5) included such change targets as: influencing legislation, changing hiring practices, helping the poor or · "recipients" to be on the boards that direct social service agencies, and eliminating racist attitudes.

Critique of the Two Movements

As these movements became increasingly clear about their own identity they began to pull apart. Soon each became the target of criticism, not only from the other but also from outside observers. They came to be seen as mutually exclusive. In some cases they actually contended against one another.

This was partly because they enlisted different adherents and focused on divergent emphases (counseling vs. action) and were competing for the same funds from the same audience and constituencies (church people), but partly too because each was essentially incomplete without the other. The arguments directed against these discrete pastoral care functions are worth enumerating.

Social Action Divorced from Pastoral Counseling

Many actionists are clearly naive when it comes to recognizing the needs people have for developing trust before they can build an effective and efficient team. Whereas the counselor may focus too much on personal relationships, the social actionist often is blind to them altogether *until* contention or lack of participation sabotages the organizing effort. One of the most frequent difficulties social action groups experience is the erosion of group effectiveness as a result of their not taking the time or making the effort to build trust or manage the needs of the individuals within the group.

Moreover, social actionists have tended not to know what to do about the emotional issues that inevitably crop up in the course of their planning and implementation efforts. When personal problems become so blatant that they cannot be denied, actionists tend to complain about them but remain befuddled as to what to do to change them.

One of us was working as a consultant with a religious group on a university campus a few years ago trying to help develop plans for an action that would be a relevant and effective response to the United States' incursion into Cambodia. Each time the group was close to making a decision about what it was going to do, the decision (or people's commitment to it) was sabotaged by a few members who began backbiting, through rumor undermining the integrity of the group and its other members. Instead of dealing directly with these interpersonal problems, the members simply redoubled their protest efforts. They tried to sidestep interpersonal difficulties through working harder.

In this particular situation the primary difficulty stemmed from competitive and provocative behavior on the part of two of the group leaders. This activist group needed help in building relationships within the organization. Working with each leader separately, we helped each one see how he characteristically dealt with the proposals and ideas of the other. Once each had perceived his own nonhelpful behavior and its negative impact on the group, we brought the two leaders together for a common session with one of us as facilitator. Each was asked to describe how he had himself acted in such a way as to unintentionally exacerbate the situation. These candid personal revelations made it possible for each to begin trusting the other and to feel less defensive and provocative toward the other, thus reducing the group tension and helping the decision-making process.

Another criticism which is often justly aimed at social actionists has reference to the "bull-in-the-china-shop" syndrome that makes many conscientious church people fretful, resistant, and angry in the presence of determined actionists. Many stories from the war period tell about actionists who aimed inflexibly at a single goal (sometimes unrealistically grandiose), laying on "guilt trips," and denying other points of view as they self-righteously pursued what they thought was correct. Such behavior is not only indecorous, it is often counterproductive.

Several times during the 60s and early 70s we were asked to work with local congregations to help eradicate racism and develop affirmative action programs. We found from bitter experience that when we started our work by blaming and attacking the people we were supposed to be changing, we only increased their resistance, making it nearly impossible even to get their attention. They then engaged in blaming and attacked us in return. They denied that problems existed. They even invented reasons for not continuing to be a part of the antiracism or affirmative action program. Conversely, we found that when we began our work with a congregation by appreciating their resources and asking them to join with us in an attempt to describe and define the problems of prejudice, discrimination, and racism, the participants were much more likely to collaborate in the problem-solving.

Furthermore, people in social action often come across as guilt makers, blaming others for racism that occurred hundreds of years ago, attacking them for the insignificant character of their response—so small in comparison to the size and scope of the problems being addressed—and putting them down for being callous toward others' problems and pain.

People in New Testament times experienced similar guilt making when they were confronted by the legalistic and authoritarian demands of religion and Empire. Tax collectors, spies, centurions, and bureaucrats were looking over everyone's shoulders demanding taxes, tributes, and allegiance. At the same time, devout teachers were daily reminding everyone not to eat this meat, not to pick that grain, be sure to give alms at prescribed times, and to keep a kosher house as well.

In Jesus' day, guilt makers were everywhere. Whenever a person thought every rule had been obeyed, every demand answered, someone was sure to come up with yet one more. It seemed as if the people would never get out from under it all. There was no way to respond to the endless burdens of the law. The people felt hopeless in the face of all those "oughts" and "shoulds."

It was in this environment that Jesus preached the good news: Life is a gift, not a demand! What one receives from the Spirit is love, joy, peace, patience, kindness, goodness, fidelity, gentleness, and self-control. One receives these by living them. To put it another way, to everyone who hears the message and accepts the gift, life has a new motivational base from which to proceed —a person is freed from viewing life as a demand or an obligation. And this means, among other things, that one is freed from seeing social action as a demand.

Pastoral Counseling Divorced from Social Action

While the social action types have been justly criticized for some of the things they have been doing, the counselors have had equally valid criticisms directed at them. Actionists have been disappointed at seeing little counseling activity in the cause of social justice. Edwin Schur, a sociologist at New York University, wrote a book entitled *The Awareness Trap: Self-Absorption Instead of Social Change** in which he takes the self-awareness movement to task, not because its ideology precludes active pursuit of social and political goals, but because an exclusive focus on the personal and interpersonal levels of human experience tends to inhibit sociopolitical action. He says that emphasis on one mode will usually be at the expense of the other. This has sometimes happened in pastoral counseling—counselors have tended to focus exclusively on emotional and interpersonal issues to the neglect of those issues of justice and forces in the environment that actually shape individual lives.

Moreover, sometimes a counselor's range of skills and focus of attention is too narrow to help the client deal with the social causes of pain. Dennis Jaffee wrote of his attempts in a youth crisis center to recognize these social factors and do something about them:

> I have become sensitive to the extreme interconnections within one's environment—including the community from which clients come, the relationships among staff, and one's helpfulness

to clients. While tradition rigorously limits the helper's role and responsibility, my work questions such limits. When one begins to see clients' dilemmas as consequences of their positions within an oppressive environment, the solutions involve direct intervention, creation of concrete alternative communities, and helping them develop a strategy of social change which will enable them to meet their legitimate needs. Rather than adjustment to a difficult situation with resignation, the goal might better be to develop a sense of personal movement and change so that a new environment can be created.*

Furthermore, the counseling movement needs to look at many of its practitioners who have too completely espoused Maslow's idea of *self*-actualization or *self-fulfillment*.† James MacGregor Burns, in his book *Leadership*, thinks that there is an overemphasis on an individual's ability to actualize himself or herself. Burns believes that self-actualization rises less from internal factors than from the interplay of the "self-actualized" with other persons, accompanied by a steady rise in tolerant understanding, an open and inclusive attitude toward them, an ability to assess themselves in "reflexive self-awareness," and a relatively rational and orderly approach to the problem:

> The most marked characteristic of self-actualizers as potential leaders goes beyond Maslow's self-actualization; it is their capacity to *learn* from others and from the environment—the capacity *to be taught*. That capacity calls for an ability to listen and be guided by others without being threatened by them, to be dependent on others but not overly dependent, to judge other persons with both affection and discrimination, to possess enough autonomy to be creative without rejecting the external influences that make for growth and relevance. Self-actualization ultimately means the ability *to lead by being led*.‡

The goal of personal growth is not independence but interdependence. When Maslow's self-actualizing principles have been put into practice in business and industry, the results are sometimes not very favorable.§ Self-actualizers often do not fit well into teams. They tend to be too aloof, loners, different from others and unable to fit into organizational activity.

However, the most powerful criticisms of self-actualization as the end product of personal growth strategies has been raised by Victor Frankl who says that if self-actualization becomes one's goal or criterion, one contradicts the self-transcendent quality of human existence itself. Frankl believes that self-actualization, like happiness, comes with the fulfillment of meaning. It is a by-product of the process of realizing or actualizing values or meanings in one's life. This process is basically self-transcendent rather than self-centered. Frankl says that a person finds self to the extent to which he or she in the first instance loses self—he decides to behave morally "for the sake of a cause to which he commits himself or for a person whom he loves, or for the sake of his God."* In short, fulfillment comes not from the pursuit of fulfillment, but from the satisfaction derived from pursuing a meaning or goal beyond the self.

Finally, while actionists may at times be too acerbic, counselors have been charged with being too compassionate. Karl Menninger in his book *Whatever Became of Sin†* addresses this well. He notes that the clergy may have overidentified with mental health professionals and failed to be as forceful as they should be in creating and maintaining viable value symbols to guide everyday life. Menninger points out that psychological problems involve value confusions just as frequently as they involve straightforward emotional and interpersonal dynamics. If people are to be mentally healthy, they must not only have techniques for coping emotionally, they must also have resources for stabilizing their value decisions. Therefore, the pastor is expected to be more than a caring presence and sustainer. Fully living out the pastoral role will also mean providing an example and guidance to those who are unable to make healthy value decisions.

Exclusive Focus on Remediation

Besides the criticism that can be brought against each of the movements, there is an argument that can be brought against both of them: counseling and social action both have often lost sight of any purpose beyond remediation. Remedies are certainly important; indeed they may be absolutely necessary before further development can occur. Both pastoral counseling and social action, however, have tended to stop there, with counselors trying to help people develop specific coping skills and actionists trying to put an end to specific injustices or inequalities. Each group thereby loses sight of certain other important goals, the necessary personal and social goals of developing such life-styles, institutions, and beliefs as can foster and encourage a more moral world. These are the goals that, held in balanced focus, can fuse counseling and action into a full and whole ministry of pastoral care. Helping individuals merely adjust to their environment or cope with their emotions stops short of providing the resources necessary for creating a better world, and stopping specific injustices or meeting the particular needs of individuals, families, or groups does little to create the incentives, attitudes, and systems that can reduce the need for future stopgap or remedial activities.

Holistic Pastoral Care

The integration of pastoral counseling and social action comes about when each sees the other as necessary to a larger and fuller end: the development of individuals *and* systems whose purposes embody faith in God, reverence for all creation, and love of neighbor. These are the concerns recognized by Paul in 1 Corinthians 12 when he talks about the body of Christ having many members and each part having a different function. No part is assumed to be better than another. Each part serves the head, which is Christ. So it is with social action and pastoral counseling: each helps make up a greater whole, each points toward the same goal, and each is under the same leadership.*

What we are saying here is that effective pastoral care involves more than social change methods learned in a school of social work, and more than therapeutic techniques learned in a department of psychology. It is faith, reverence, and love infusing the symbiotic relationship between systems and persons that makes the several interventions uniquely Christian. Knowledge of change technology, a sense of justice, a supportive demeanor—these are important, but not enough. Holistic pastoral care does not engage in change for change's sake, nor does it stop at an eye for an eye or at creating an environment of trust. At its root is a purpose which includes these but goes beyond them: to help every person *and* the environment glorify God and fulfill creation.

Bringing the Movements Together

As the counseling and social action movements came into conflict, church leaders recognized the need to identify their common roots and find their essential compatibility. Howard Clinebell, a seminary teacher of pastoral counseling, joined with Harvey Seifert, a teacher of social ethics, to write *Personal Growth and Social Change** in an effort to bring these two strands of ministry together. Other experiments and writings came into existence with a view to similarly integrating pastoral counseling and social action. Perhaps the most notable effort in this regard was the project funded by the W. Clement and Jessie V. Stone Foundation called the Ministry in the Seventies Project. Rhea Gray and Billy Short originally framed its formative concept: "to focus primarily on the pastoral counseling movement, which had been on the cutting edge of both the church's ministry and of theological education . . . , but now seemed to be in a 'cul de sac,' allowing history to pass it by." Sixteen projects were established with the hope of "bringing about some integration of the concerns for both pastoral care and social action."† Significant learnings resulted from these experiments in integrating counseling and action, some of which were summarized by Daniel Day Williams in a chapter of the book, *Explorations in Ministry.*‡

Williams noted four convictions emerging from these striking experiments in ministry. First, he pointed out that there was a major shift away from concern with individual person-to-person relationships and toward ministry within groups for the sake of groups, meeting group problems, and with a view to the group's engagement with the major structures of power in institutions. Williams found this shift from individual to group ministries to be startling and radical, noting that the context of pastoral ministry is now more within groups and their processes as they look toward liberation, reconciliation, and reconstruction within the corporate forms of life.

This movement from individual to group ministries was a first step toward the fusion of pastoral counseling and social action in holistic pastoral care. Whereas social action had previously focused on groups (usually large, corporate structures), counseling had focused on the individual. Pastoral counseling was now taking the initiative to unite the two forms of ministry. Certainly these experiments did not go far enough at the time—many of them using small groups only in order to focus on individual problems—but it was clearly a significant step toward integration of the movements.

Second, Williams pointed to the growing understanding on the part of counselors that individual stress and the bondage it produces cannot be fathomed apart from the social structures in which individuals live. Family, communities, nations, and world society have an impact on—and in turn are impacted by—the individual.

Third, he said that changing social structures for the sake of persons involves skills and strategies which have to do with the dynamics of group interaction: "Social change requires cooperative action. The pastor is not only a resource for meeting individual problems but also a leader of a community within communities, seeking to aid in the renewal of life, removal of injustice, and healing of the spirit. Individuals must find freedom and purpose in participation in the common life and its problems."*

Finally, Williams felt it essential for Christian ministers and teachers to achieve a new identification with those engaged in struggles for social justice. Pastoral care that is directed to people who are hurting, wherever they may be, calls for movement beyond the boundaries of class and race that exist in local congregations in order to encounter modes of life different from one's own. Out of this encounter comes not only new understandings of those who are oppressed, but also new styles and strategies of helping that can significantly aid the counselor or actionist.

Since those early experiments, other groups have begun to address the same integration questions, thereby reversing the strong tendency toward compartmentalization of spiritual growth, pastoral counseling, social action, liturgical renewal, and Christian education—as if they were all separate ministries rather than aspects of the warp and woof that makes up the whole cloth of the pastoral care of persons. A few of these current experiments are worth further exploration: The Whole Church Project developed by the Institute for Advanced Pastoral Studies in Bloomfield Hills, Michigan; Well-Spring, a mission of the Church of The Savior in Washington, D.C.; and Eagles, an interdenominational ministry in Dayton, Ohio.†

Each of the above experiments, as well as the Ministry in the Seventies Project, can be seen as attempts to reintegrate counseling and action. Thus integrated, the two disciplines become part of a holistic pastoral care, a united ministry that reconciles the false antagonisms of the recent past. When pastoral counseling and social action join forces they work together in support of both individuals and groups. They (1) develop a framework of meaning relevant to all aspects of life; (2) incorporate people into a moral world; and (3) empower people to build, reform, and shape those aspects of the world that lead to the collapse of that moral world.

Don Browning, in his book *The Moral Context of Pastoral Care,** explains how the church has done this throughout history. He points out that it is the purpose of ministry to help form the character of a people, seeking to reform those value systems which are in disarray by forming collectives for action to support and sustain those in the reform movements.

The Common Goal

This is the heart of the integration of pastoral counseling and social action. They come together under the common goal of pastoral care, which is incomplete if either counseling or action alone is emphasized. William Clebsch and Charles Jaekle, in their book *Pastoral Care in Historical Perspective,* have identified the four aspects of care as healing, sustaining, guiding, and reconciling:

> *Healing* is that function in which a representative Christian person helps a debilitated person to be restored to a condition of wholeness, on the assumption that this restoration achieves also a new level of spiritual insight and welfare. *Sustaining* consists of helping a hurting person to endure and to transcend a circumstance in which restoration to his former condition is remote or impossible. *Guiding* consists of assisting perplexed persons to make confident choices when such choices are viewed as affecting the present or future state of the soul. *Reconciling* functions to reestablish broken relationships between man and fellowman and between man and God.†

Holistic pastoral care focuses on healing, sustaining, guiding, and reconciling. To make a whole ministry, all four functions must be called into play. Otherwise the ministry is incomplete. Counseling has tended to focus on healing, sustaining, and guiding of the individual. Social action has focused on reconciling groups and changing institutional structures. In holistic pastoral care, the two are brought together as healing, sustaining, guiding, and reconciling are directed to both individuals and groups.

Collaborative Methods

Both counselors and actionists use collaborative change methods. Collaborative methods are those in which the helper intentionally works with others both inside and outside the target systems in order to devise improvements that are mutually satisfactory. The helper and the one(s) helped are co-laborers. The predicament and concerns of others are accepted as valid, and those in ministry join with others affected by the problem in order to find innovative possibilities for improvement.

Collaborative pastoral care is based on certain assumptions. In using the approach counselors and actionists both assume the basic value and potential for health of the systems or persons to be changed. Collaborative effort also assumes that change which is the deepest and lasts the longest is change in which both the changer and the persons in the systems to be changed agree on the fact that there is a problem and choose to work together in trying to find a solution.

The police department in a city south of Los Angeles had received a large amount of bad publicity from a reporter who heard a lieutenant give a speech to local merchants on how to identify and deal with potential shoplifters. The officer's racist remarks and suggestions for dealing with minorities were shocking to many in the community. Instead of joining picket lines in front of the police station, however, the interdenominational ministry with which we were working offered its services to help train police personnel and generally raise the consciousness of the entire force. Rather than join the attack, we offered help. Our offer of services was accepted and the church agency collaborated with the police department in helping to change the behavior and attitude of its employees. Called into play were ministries not only of reconciliation, but also of healing, sustaining, and guiding.

Ministry that involves both counseling and action—hence holistic pastoral care—assumes the need to establish an atmosphere of trust at the outset. An environment in which the participants sense that it is safe for them to share openly and to work together on the issue is essential for every kind of social change except that which is coercive and willing to remain dependent on force to create and maintain change. Once a climate of safety has been established, the group or individual can then gather information on the nature of the problem, separate impossible problems from those about which something can be done, consider alternative strategies for these "workable problems," and develop an action plan.

In the case of the police department with the racist policies for dealing with potential shoplifters, the department knew it had a problem because it was under attack from several quarters in the city. To keep "laying it on" them would only have made the officers and their leaders more defensive. The initial approach of the interdenominational ministry was to communicate to the police department that it understood their difficulty and that it wanted to help them deal with the dual problems of its image in the community and the racism manifest in its people and policies. Once the ministry had worked with the department to establish a climate of safety and trust, the two were able to interact and collaborate in naming specific, workable problems and in jointly developing strategies to deal with them.

Parenthetically it should be noted that there are times, both in counseling ministries and social action ministries, when collaborative methods may be inappropriate. The counselor who finds that the clients are about to do harm to themselves or others may decide to intervene with pressure or even force. There are occasions as well when the actionist may decide to intervene for social change using political power and pressure. This is especially true in those situations where collaboration has been tried and failed because the people in power will not join in a collaborative mode, or where the government has already established contest strategies (voting or trying a case in court) as the appropriate decision-making mode, or where a group is protecting itself against unfair and unjust incursions. In such instances noncollaborative methodologies may indeed be more appropriate. But our point is that the usual and preferred methods of both counseling and social action are and should be collaborative.

The Primacy of Grace

It should also be pointed out that social action and pastoral counseling share the same fundamental assumption that, even as

God demands radical obedience, so God also "forgives all your iniquity and heals all your diseases" (Ps. 103:3). As pastoral counselors we are sensitive to the fact that too heavy an emphasis on judgment is not only inadequate theology, it is therapeutically ineffective. God's claim for obedience must be seen as inseparable from God's gift. Daniel Day Williams describes forgiveness as

> God's action in standing by the sinner and reconstituting the relationship broken by wrongdoing. Sin is not only the breaking of the divine law; it is personal estrangement, it is the separation of man from the true source of his being. It is the life created for love twisted into the life of lovelessness. The gift of God is his powerful invasion of the disordered life we create for ourselves, and his persuasive power to set us in a right relation again.*

The social actionist who sees that society's leaders and the systems in which they work are inadequate must also emphasize God's grace and goodness.

Christian pastoral care assumes that God demands obedience, chastises disobedience, and reestablishes relationship through forgiveness. Social action has had a tendency to make "the other" an enemy—whether that other be a group (Ku Klux Klan), a business (Nestlé), or a place (suburbia). Pastoral counseling has had a tendency to overlook the existence of corporate evil. Both social action and pastoral counseling at their best, however, assume the reality of sin *and* grace, good *and* evil in the world and in people. The ministry of holistic pastoral care believes there is hope for positive change. Neither counseling nor action assumes any person, relationship, or community to be "beyond grace."

2. Identifying Action Resources

The goals of pastoral care are more difficult to achieve where pastors operate as if all people were the same or have the same needs. There is a tendency among some pastors to see their congregations as "a group of conservatives who wouldn't touch social action ministries with a ten-foot pole," or "a congregation of people who are already overextended in many voluntary activities," or "a collection of insecure and tentative individuals." While such generalizations may be descriptive of some persons in the congregation—even a majority—they do not adequately or accurately describe each individual. In our experience most congregations are far more complex, including a mixture of people who are both liberal and conservative, caring and not so caring, involved and not so involved, healthy and unhealthy, mature and immature.

If pastoral care is to be relevant to the people and their situation, the leadership of the congregation must be aware of and responsive to the variety of needs and persons actually represented. Such awareness and responsiveness may well begin with an effort to name the variety of gifts as well as problems that are present, and then proceed to the development of programs relevant to them. Our experience has led us to describe the pastoral care differences found within a church in terms of five categories of people: persons needing remedial care, persons feeling a pinch, persons already involved in caring ministries, persons wanting to do more, and persons not ready to get involved. (There is also a sixth category, to be dealt with at least implicitly in chapter 6, namely those who work against constructive social change.)

People Needing Remedial Care

There are many people in every congregation who at any given time are hurting severely because of crises confronting them personally. In every person's life at some time or another events occur and circumstances arise that make it impossible for the individual to have energy left for anything other than the personal battle for physical or emotional survival. The death of a loved one, breakup of a marriage, loss of a job, mental illness, severe frustration over one's children, vocational uncertainty, confusion about the meaning of one's life—all are illustrative of the kinds of problems confronting these people who are themselves in need of remedial pastoral care.

People going through such experiences are so caught up in personal pain and situational difficulties that they do not have full access to their own resources for ministry to others. Their attention and activities are directed instead toward their own emotional and physical survival, and these concerns must be dealt with before such persons can be set free to assume and address concerns beyond themselves. For persons in this state pastoral care is properly directed toward relief of the various physical ills, anxieties, or inner conflicts blocking their access to a full, free, and abundant life.

It is not our intention here to address the care processes indicated for people in this state. There are other books in this series that the reader should find helpful in this regard, especially *Pastoral Care and Counseling in Grief and Separation* by Wayne Oates and *Crisis Counseling* by Howard Stone.*

People Feeling a Pinch

While some people are in such an emotional or physical state as to need concentrated remedial care themselves, others are hindered from full functioning and appreciation of life because of difficulties that stem from social or environmental causes. These people may variously describe their experience in terms of alienation, lack of hope, boredom, injustice, or oppression. Perhaps they are oppressed by sexism at home, at church, or at work; or are bored and alienated in a "dead end" job; or are suffering from relative (as over against abject) poverty or racial discrimination.

William Ryan gives an example of involved welfare mothers
who, in consequence of their immediate needs, were motivated to
change a department of social services. Note that for them part
of the pinch is—in addition to their children's needs—their own
powerlessness:

> On the welfare front we are beginning to see the effects of the
> exercise of power as well as the slight shift in that balance of
> power which has been achieved by welfare rights groups. It is
> a rare pleasure to observe the realization dawning among a
> group of welfare mothers that their potential for disruption and
> embarrassment through plain physical presence of numbers
> (often almost comically menacing) is a source of *power* that
> they can use in their own interest. When a welfare supervisor,
> after a day or week of being surrounded by sitting-in mothers
> who are obviously there, not for fun, but to *get* something for
> their children; to *force* out of that web of desks, and papers,
> and typewriters, and desk calendars, and file cabinets a couple
> of pair of pants, some new shoes, and maybe some sheets and
> pillow cases—when that welfare supervisor starts passing out
> checks or vouchers to the mothers, it is really something to be-
> hold. Those mothers have received a sliver of power, a tiny
> scrap of control of their own lives, and they will never forget it.*

Feeling a pinch is not limited just to persons concerned with
sheer survival. Many nonsurvival pinches also motivate the development of social movements. Movements for the conservation
of energy, for example, are generated by a shortage of gasoline
for cars. Movements for equal rights develop from the humilia-
tion women experience at the hands of people who belittle their
competence. Farmers join forces to put pressure on the government or on the market for economic relief.

Sometimes those who are experiencing a pinch are aware of
the pain, but not yet clear about the cause. Studs Terkel lets one
such person, Grace Clements, speak for herself:

> Before the union came in, all I did was do my eight hours, col-
> lect my paycheck, and go home, did my housework, took care
> of my daughter, and went back to work. I had no outside in-
> terests. . . . You just lived to live. Since I became active in the
> union, I've become active in politics, in the community, in
> legislative problems. I've been to Washington on one or two
> trips. I've been to Springfield. That has given me more of an
> incentive for life. . . . I see others, I'm sad. They just come to
> work, do their work, go home, take care of their home, and
> come back to work. Their conversation is strictly about their
> family and meals. They live each day for itself and that's about

it. . . . My whole attitude on the job has changed since the union came in. Now I would like to be a union counselor or work for the Office of Economic Opportunity. I work with humans as grievance committee chairman. They come to you angry, they come to you hurt, they come to you puzzled. You have to make life easier for them.*

Persons who are dissatisfied but unable to specify the cause of their dissatisfaction may be difficult to organize. These may be individuals who have not verbalized their complaints in the past, but have nevertheless indicated that they are indeed feeling a pinch. Or they may be persons whose complaints about life are expressed in a general or nonspecific way. For example, they may complain loudly about the way city council operates but without detailing their specific gripes.

In Southern California in the 1960s a group of fifteen women discovered among themselves a common denominator of mutual interests. They referred to their broad umbrella of common concerns as "women's issues": getting financial credit for a divorced woman; feeling put down as a woman in this society; feeling offended by and left out of a church liturgy that uses exclusively masculine gender words. Because of their awareness of these common issues and mutual concerns these women were able to come together to explore the possibility of providing support for one another—and later became an action group.

People Wanting to Do More

There are people in every congregation who are looking for greater fulfillment in their own lives. They are aware that they have been given much, and are thankful for the abundance they have received. These people are currently not involved in the larger community, or are active in only a limited way. Out of gratitude, out of a sense of what they have to share, they desire to give or to help. Usually they do not experience the need for counseling or for a "support" group. They simple want to do more.

In a suburb of Los Angeles, a small group of women were not content with sitting at home after the house was cleaned, the children delivered to school, and the shopping done. As one of the women put it: "We have ourselves on our hands." Playing bridge and tennis were enjoyable activities but hardly fulfilling. A paid career was neither needed nor wanted. As much for their own sanity as for the needs they saw in the community these women organized themselves into a political action group that became a formidable power both at City Hall and throughout the area.

They addressed themselves first to repressive dress and grooming codes at the junior and senior high schools. Once they had achieved all they thought they could in that area, they tackled the problem of white racism. With ever-increasing skills and competence the group helped local congregations examine how the church itself was contributing to the problem and what could be done about it. As a part of such involvement the women helped elect a candidate to the Los Angeles School Board. They formed dialogue groups encompassing people who otherwise lived apart in separate black and white communities.

Not all of their actions were successful by any means. Some ended in setbacks, some in feelings of futility. Yet much of their involvement proved rewarding. Most of the women felt a great increase in their sense of power and self-esteem. They were meeting their own needs for personal fulfillment as they faced the challenges about them.

While some of these women wanted to do more because of emptiness or boredom in their own lives, many chose to become involved in social action out of a sense of gratitude. For some it was clearly a case of thankfulness that they had received the wonderful gift of God's act of grace in Christ. For others their gratitude had a more naturalistic base in such specific gifts as economic security, personal health, or social success. While most responded actively to what had been given them, a few responded from a sense of guilt. In some cases there was a mixture of all these various motives.

Pam Conrod once wrote of the motives she and her husband may have had as they decided to sponsor a refugee family:

> My husband and I sponsored a Vietnamese family in the sum-
> mer of 75, when the first boat people fled their country and
> came to the United States. Occasionally we speculate, fruit-
> lessly, on what motivated us to do it. Certainly, we felt com-
> passion; every evening on TV we watched these homeless peo-

ple in their refugee existence at Camp Pendleton. Was it guilt that made us do it? My husband, although he had never gone to Vietnam or seen combat, had been drafted and had participated in the war in a peripheral, stateside way. Guilt? There was no blood on his hands, but yes, there was a bad taste in his mouth and mine. And as we sat one night in our neat suburban home with our healthy children, our color TV, our indoor plumbing, and our tropical fish tank, we knew we had it good, and we were both moved by the same compulsion to reach out.*

Seldom, if ever, are people clear or singleminded in their motivations. The task of the pastor working with these people is to help them to appreciate and articulate what they are grateful for and to understand the connection between this gratitude and the variety of ways in which they may respond.

People Already Involved in Caring Ministries

There is in most congregations a large contingent of people already involved in organized or individual caring activities. Some may be addressing issues of special concern—hunger, racism, the handicapped—and be in need of support, recognition, and affirmation. Others may be equally involved but have little or no need of recognition and support.

Many Christians are independently engaged in caring ministries that are not organized by or centered in the institutional church. It is our contention that these ministries are just as valid and important as those that are officially accredited as church work. Too often local congregations do not recognize adequately those acts of caring that go on outside the structures of an official church committee or action group. We propose that local churches not only support and recognize the people who are thus working for the kingdom apart from the institutional church, but also find a way to recognize, support, and account for the many ministries that are actually deployed through channels other than official church agencies. We shall have occasion to refer to this in subsequent chapters.

These extrachurch ministries of caring take many forms:

Martha is an old-time "peacemaker." A pacifist who joined peace marches during the Vietnam era, she is a member of the Women's International League for Peace and Freedom. During the height of the national interest in racial issues she also ran for election to the school board on a probusing platform.

Michael is a young attorney, about thirty. For the past two years he has been giving "pro bono" service to an organization of poor people seeking to deal with slum landlords.

Carlos is the vice-president of a savings and loan association in a medium-sized metropolitan community. He has been in conflict with his boss and several board members over the association's policy of "red-lining" (deciding not to make home loans in high-risk poverty sections of town).

Karen is a teacher who has devoted many hours to the church's Social Concerns Committee. She reads all the newsletters from denominational headquarters and tries to do all the really exciting programs recommended. Her recent activities have included delivering meals-on-wheels for the elderly, advocating legislation for state and federal aid to hungry people, and supporting the United Farm Workers Union.

Sometimes the people engaged in such ministries see themselves as fighting for high principles, struggling to help the world's poor, or trying to uphold a special ministry that inevitably carries with it a measure of conflict and dissension. Often these people have resigned themselves to a minority status in the membership of the church. Sometimes they see themselves as a "burr under the saddle," provoking the church to action. Others, however, may perceive them as "activists," a threat to church stability that makes such organizational activities as fund raising or new member recruitment more difficult.

These people already involved in action ministries sometimes have a unique set of needs to which pastoral care may be addressed. These needs actually represent opportunities not only for the pastor's ministry but also for the people themselves to minister to one another. The needs may result from or be identified in terms of how the people are feeling:

Feeling Isolated. Since evangelism in many a local church means simply getting more members, the congregation, consciously or unconsciously, often defines itself simply in terms of worship, family-oriented experiences, and spiritual growth. People who join the church in order to serve the needs of a global family, or who see governmental policy as central to their vision of ministry, often experience themselves as a minority. The church may reject them or they may isolate themselves.

Feeling up against Overwhelming Odds. These people are often sensitive to media messages about the magnitude of the world's problems. Even the most dedicated Christian response can seem futile compared to the world's unending needs.

Feeling Frustrated by the Lack of Success. It is difficult to maintain the morale of any enterprise without the occasional experiences of success. Out of necessity social action persons often choose difficult projects that address huge problems—world hunger or nuclear proliferation—with resources that seem infinitesimal in comparison to the needs. And sometimes social action projects are so poorly conceptualized that small victories seem inadequate. To organize with a view to ending poverty in our lifetime or achieving a new economic order is to frame expectations in global terms and make action at the local level seem void of success.

Feeling Burdened by Oughts and Shoulds. Some people in social action seem to have an especially punishing conscience. They look at the world of suffering and experience guilt because of their own relative wealth, position, or circumstance. While this guilt is sometimes appropriate, often it is an inappropriate response to the reality of their lives or what can be done to change the world situation.

Feeling Unsupported by the Church. Compared to the resources and attention given the building program, the organ fund, and the children's educational program, the social action budget usually seems meager and slighted. Further, the people administering it often feel that the lion's share of attention and recognition is reserved for programs of inner growth and personal relations while only minuscule notice is given to mission and social concerns.

Feeling "Exposed" by Risk Taking on Positions of Public Policy. Working for change means threatening the status quo, the relatively comfortable conditions in which many of the congregation's members live. For this reason the advocate for change is often perceived as a source of threat by other members in the same congregation.

Feeling Overwhelmed by So Many Issues. There are so many social problems and they all demand attention. Denomination and church leaders rarely help to select the issue of highest priority. Instead, the chairperson of the social action committee receives announcements each month of several new, competing programs appealing for the group's attention.

Feeling Drained by Solving Somebody Else's Problems. Since the usual definition of social action is to meet the needs of other people (Indians, farm workers, hurricane and earthquake victims), one can spend lots of energy without getting refilled.

People Not Ready to Get Involved

Finally, it is only realistic to recognize that there are people who are neither seriously hurting, nor feeling a pinch, nor wanting to do more, nor already involved. Sometimes we ungraciously regard these people as those who are just going along for the ride.

It certainly would be noble to work long and hard at attempting to get these people into action, and a good deal of attention has been given to such attempts.* While much has been written about how to wake up those who choose to do nothing, even more energy has been spent by pastors—and by church committees at the local, regional, and national levels—anguishing over what might be done to utilize these unlikely candidates for ministry. It is our thesis, however, that only limited resources should be expended on church people who are simply not ready to get involved.

An Italian economist at the beginning of this century propounded a theory now known as Pareto's Law. It states that when a collection of items or activities are arranged in order of value, 80 percent of the value would come from only 20 percent of the items or activities, while the remaining 20 percent of the value would come from 80 percent of the items or activities. Thus, it is likely that 20 percent of your files are used 80 percent of the time. Eighty percent of the income from your church probably comes from 20 percent of the members. Eighty percent of the work gets done by 20 percent of the members, and, perhaps, 80 percent of the building use is carried out in 20 percent of the building.

Applied to pastoral care, Pareto's Law might suggest that instead of devoting 80 percent of your time and energy to situations where there is only a 20 percent return (whether to church, society, or the individual), you reverse the ratio and spend only 20 percent of your resources where the likelihood of return is going to be small. In making this recommendation we are not proposing a kind of pastoral care triage. (*Triage* is a word of French origin meaning to cull out or set aside certain items or members of a class as inferior. The principle is now used not only in medical contexts but also in connection with hungry people or mentally ill people whom the government writes off as hopeless so that policy administrators can utilize their scarce resources instead for persons who are perceived to be salvageable.)

Our proposal is not tied to such all-or-nothing schemes. We are advocating only that one not devote large amounts of money, time, and emotional energy in investments not likely to pay off.

A certain amount of "venture capital" is always appropriate, but not to the detriment of other ministries deemed more likely to be responsible to the church's pastoral care.

Neither is our proposal made out of ignorance of the parable of the lost sheep. That parable was probably not meant as a guilt trip to be laid on people who are already overworked. Its message—that the lost have a good shepherd who will care for them —is clearly one of grace, not of demand. But a call to ministry is also heard—appropriately—in the parable. This focus on the one lost, however, is not a call to be irresponsible toward the remaining ninety-nine. Jesus clearly tells us that the shepherd left the flock in an uninhabited grassland which "is not a specially perilous or desolate place, but their usual pasture, in which they are properly tended. He does not neglect them, but for the moment he is absorbed in the recovery of the lost."* It would be quite wrong to conclude from this parable that it is appropriate regularly to devote the majority of one's attention and effort to lost causes. The pastor is indeed concerned for the lost, but not at the expense of the ninety-nine.

How might we identify these persons who are "not ready to get off their duff"? People who simply are not ready to get involved are likely to be the persons who do not show up at meetings, even after being carefully encouraged; who argue continually about almost every caring idea proposed; who rarely show up at Sunday morning worship; and who say they will do a task for the church but then fail to follow through.

When it comes to identifying resources for social action within the congregation these five (or six) categories may prove helpful. The rest of this book will be addressed to the question of how to engage in holistic pastoral care (counseling *and* action) those people who are feeling a pinch, want to do more, or are already involved in some kind of caring ministries either inside or outside the institutional church.

3. Starting Action Groups

Not long ago Al Jones, the pastor of First Methodist Church, called together fourteen people who he thought might be interested in forming a Social Concerns Committee. Only after the meeting did he discover that Marv and Judy Lester had a retarded child of their own and that Pat Fisher's sister had a child with severe emotional and learning disabilities—and only then did he begin to understand why members of the group had expressed such strong interest in developing programs relevant to the needs of families with uniquely difficult children. During the meeting, Bob Christian on the other hand had not been at all interested in devoting time and energy to what he called "social service"; he preferred an organizing, demonstrating, and lobbying effort to persuade the County Board of Supervisors that they should outlaw the use of firearms for any purpose other than law enforcement. Most of the other people in attendance were simply confused between these two forcefully expressed positions; given the alternatives, they hardly knew where to begin, because they saw many possible areas of involvement and had no notion of how to go about deciding, much less which alternative to choose.

Because they could not agree on a program priority, the group decided instead simply to read and discuss their denominational publications in social action, and report on them to the congregation. Their inability to find an activity that could be meaningful to them all left each of them unfulfilled, and they gradually began to reduce their scale of participation. Some even quit altogether. The situation was obviously confusing. Had the pastor been more careful, and given greater thought to whom he would invite in the first place, he might have had greater success. Certainly there would have been fewer hurt feelings.

Selecting Participants

It is important, in selecting someone to be invited to participate in an action group, that leaders draw wisely on both their experience and their intuition. It is unwise to assume that whoever shows up simply on the basis of a general announcement is a potential recruit—or, for that matter, that whoever may have previously indicated some interest in an action program will be a likely candidate. Leaders who first recall what they already know about individuals can often discard the names of some least likely to fit in with such a group.

Two methods have proved particularly useful for getting additional information about persons who might seem qualified for an invitation to participate in a pastoral care project. The first is the tried and true method of calling on people in their homes. The second involves the use of study groups.

Home Visitation

With regard to home visitation, we recommend that you (perhaps with the help of a few trained laypersons) call on a variety of people to determine their readiness for and possible interest in fuller ministry. As you begin this process, skip people who are already heavily involved in other church ministries, leaders in the official board, buildings and grounds committee, church school, or women's fellowship. These people, who are probably already heavily committed to other forms of ministry, may find new involvements overly taxing, competing for their time, strength, and interest with what they are already doing. The key word here is the word *heavily* involved. You may identify some persons who serve on only one committee or board. If they are committed to no more than two or three nights a month in structured church activities, we would consider them—from the standpoint of prior demands—acceptable candidates for further activity. If, however, they are involved in more than three regular church programs or committees, it may prove difficult to sustain their attention and participation. A safe rule of thumb is that no person be expected or invited to join in church activities on more than two nights per week.

In an experiment one time we asked the most active members of the church to join us in a social action project; we even asked that a majority of the church council, session, or vestry participate. That was a mistake. These persons were already stretched to the limit; they had heavy commitments just in seeing to it that the church ran smoothly and efficiently. At times these commitments hindered their ability to participate in the social action effort. These active people, central figures in the governing body of the congregation, saw themselves to be representatives of others and policy makers for the congregation rather than leaders in the implementation of ministry.

It is wise to get the approval of key boards and committees in the church before attempting to recruit their members for direct participation. People in these key functional units serve best, while they are in those jobs, as authorizers of ministry rather than implementers of ministry.

Once you decide on whom you will call, prepare a schedule of questions to guide the interview with these potential participants in caring ministries. It is not necessary to have the questions written down or to ask them in a rigid sequence or abrupt question-and-answer format. Making the interview formal puts people off and discourages their interest in conversing. It is helpful, however, for you to know before you begin what you will be looking for and to have a clear sense of what you want to learn as you talk with the people. Five questions have suggested themselves as worth keeping in mind while you or your callers engage in dialogue with the people of the congregation: (1) Why are you a member of this congregation? (2) In what ways are you already personally involved in Christian ministry within the family, the community, and the church? (3) Where are the growing edges in your life? What issues, problems, hopes, and ideas are impacting you, leading you to want to be more caring, loving, mature, and competent? (4) What do you think motivates Christians to be of service to others? (5) What motivates you to be involved in the caring ministries in which you are already engaged?

People seem to have the greatest difficulty with the second question: about current involvement in Christian ministry. Whether we like it or not, most people interpret this question either as having reference only to what they do at the church or as being relevant only to persons who have chosen full-time, professional Christian service as their vocation. It is helpful to point out that Christian ministry means more than just what one does at church or under church auspices. Christian ministry can include parents' nurture of their children, the efforts of business persons to provide a better work environment, efforts of members of labor unions to make a better union, the moral leadership provided by Christian laypersons who serve on community boards, or work with groups such as Friends in Service to Humanity, Meals-on-Wheels, and the Red Cross. Getting people to think about the varieties of services and leadership they are already providing will help them answer this question about ministry in a way that will give you or the callers the most useful information concerning their potential for involvement in an action group.

Study Groups

You can also discover more about potential "recruits" by holding a study group, or a series of study groups, in which people do a good deal of sharing with respect to their real needs. Using this approach, the pastor does not have to be as careful—as in actually starting an action group—about the mix of people originally invited. Advance screening is not as crucial.

We recommend a six-session format for these study groups. Each meeting should include opportunities for worship, individual silent meditation, study of the Scriptures, and personal exchange among the participants. The optimum size for such a study group is from eight to fourteen people. A smaller group may be perceived as too intimate, a larger group as too bulky to allow for interpersonal exchange and mutual learning.

Each session should focus on a specific topic or theme. Be clear before each session what it is you would like to learn about each of the participants and what you would hope each of them might learn from the study experience. To clarify your purposes it may be helpful to write out a specific set of learning goals for the participants, and perhaps another set for the leader. The whole series of study sessions should be directed towards developing a framework of meaning for potential caring ministers. Thus, you will be starting to help the members of your congregation understand the biblical imperatives that call Christians into action and to discover such meanings and needs in their own lives as will support and direct their involvements in building, shaping, and developing a more moral world.

In addition to clarifying the learning goals for these sessions you should be clear about the activities and procedures that will be used to help you and the group members reach those goals. The agenda suggested here, which can easily be supplemented or enriched,* is not spelled out completely. Only one key exercise is suggested for each session. It will be important for your own meetings that you design each session with a view to your particular purposes and people, perhaps following the general format: (1) Short statement by leader describing the purpose and procedures of the session; (2) opening worship and prayer; (3) key exercise; (4) evaluation of the session; and (5) closing prayers.

SESSION 1

Leader's goal: to discover the participants' understandings of certain biblical imperatives.

Participants' goal: to reflect on and verbalize biblical understandings of a moral world.

Key exercise:

Distribute to all participants copies of these biblical passages: Isa. 2:4; Ezek. 34:27, 29; Luke 1:51–53; Rev. 21:1–4.

Instruct the participants to reflect on each of these passages and write a brief paragraph describing concretely what it will look like when the passage is fulfilled in the lives of all people—especially Blacks, Hispanics, Orientals, Native Americans, and third-world people. Take one passage at a time and ask each person to share his or her written paragraph with the entire group.

Discuss each passage in the light of these diverse descriptions. Strive to find a single word to characterize each passage.†

SESSION 2

Leader's goal: to discover the participants' understandings of the church.

Participants' goal: to reflect on and verbalize their theological understandings of the church.

Key exercise:

Explain that an image is a representation or a description, and provide several examples of images of the church. For example, I feel that the church is like:

—the sun after a storm
—a family during a holiday
—a subway stop
—Congress
—a filling station.

Give each participant a pencil and a 3″ x 5″ card. Ask them to write out their response as they complete the following statement: "I feel my church is like . . . ."

Then ask each participant to respond once again using a 3″ x 5″ card, by completing the following statement: "I wish my church were more like . . . ."

Display two sheets of newsprint, one headed IS and the other WISH. Invite persons to call out their written responses. Record the responses on one of the sheets of newsprint.

Ask the group to reflect on the two lists and attempt to identify any major areas in which there are differences between what is and what is desired.

Ask the group to recall and suggest biblical images of the church. Record these on yet another sheet of newsprint. Some of the following images may emerge (or even be suggested to stimulate further activity):

Household of faith	Salt of the earth
Body of Christ	Teacher
Sheep	Preacher
Light of the world	Baptizer
Chosen people	Healer

Invite the group to compare and contrast the list of biblical images of the church with their own contemporary images developed earlier.*

SESSION 3

Leader's goal: to discover the participants' understandings of their response to the biblical imperatives.

Participants' goal: to get more in touch with their own inner life.

Key exercise:

Provide the participants with a pencil and piece of paper. Ask them during a time of quiet and reflection to be aware of their actual relationship with Christ and to write down any thoughts that occur.

After allowing about ten minutes for reflection, read aloud Luke 9:1–6 and 10–13a. Before reading, though, tell the participants that somewhere in the middle of this well-known passage, at a certain point where Jesus addresses us with a demand or question, you will simply stop the reading and invite them to continue the dialogue with Christ in their own words by writing out their response to his directive. They may then—having written their own response—in fantasy continue by writing out the response they envision Christ making to them. This fantasy dialogue can continue through as many as eight or ten exchanges between the people and Christ.

The people are then encouraged to share as they wish from their written dialogue with Christ.*

SESSION 4

Leader's goal: to discover the participants' need levels.

Participants' goal: to explore and better understand what motivates them.

Key exercise:

Ask the participants to sketch (with colored chalk or charcoal on newsprint) a picture of what they remember to be their earliest success. Some might remember the first fish they caught, others their first success at riding a bike. Ask the participants to share their art with the group.

Ask the group to list on the following Satisfactions Chart (provide one chart for each person) as many as twelve achievements, successes, or moments of which they were proud in their life,

SATISFACTIONS CHART

Successes	I was with other people	I did it myself	I was in charge of what happened	I got recognition	I felt accom-plishment	I felt close to another person	I had an impact on a person or group
1							
2							
3							
4							
5							
6							
7							
8							
9							
10							
11							
12							
TOTALS							

trying to list two from childhood and adolescence and the rest from adulthood. Ask that they not list among their successes getting married, graduating, or having a baby—unless of course there were particular circumstances that made these events peculiarly special or unique accomplishments.

After listing the twelve achievements, each person is to check any box or boxes that may fit the particular experience. Several of the boxes—or even all of them—may apply to any given success.

Once the Satisfactions Chart is filled out participants can begin to note areas where they have personal needs and how these needs are being successfully satisfied. If, for example, all a person's checkmarks fall under one category, that person may have very high needs in that area. If the checks are rather evenly spread out across all seven categories, that person's needs are likely not high in any single area. The important thing to note in this connection is not whether one is "hung up" on a certain area, but where one is getting satisfaction from one's accomplishments—and then seek to fashion experiences through which one can continue to find satisfaction.

SESSION 5

Leader's goal: to discover more about the participants' value systems.

Participants' goal: to learn about values and how they function in one's own life.

Key exercise:

The Values Chart below (have a copy for each person) will help them know whether their choices are just value-indicators or in fact full-fledged, high-flying, genuine values. Tell the participants there are variations in the degree to which we cherish the various values we hold.

To make a Values Chart is to make a document worth keeping for repeated reference. It can remind us that most of our beliefs or actions rarely fit the criteria of a genuine value. It can also suggest steps that can be taken to develop stronger and clearer values.

VALUES CHART

Issues	Key Words	Processes						
		1	2	3	4	5	6	7
1								
2								
3								
4								
5								
6								
7								
8								
9								
10								

Ask the participants to list on the Values Chart some general issues they currently have feelings about, such as corruption in politics or business, water and air pollution, population control, race relations, a specific election, a community problem. Do not confine the list to just the illustratively mentioned issues. List rather any issues that deeply concern the participants. Ask them to think of what affects them personally and as members of their community. List these issues in random sequence on the left-hand side of the Values Chart. Next to each issue, write a few key words that summarize a position on that issue.

Distribute to each participant the following list of questions, pointing out that these seven questions put before us the seven processes in which we may be involved in relation to any given issue, the seven processes of values clarification. With respect to each listed issue read the entire series of seven questions. Wherever the response to a question is positive, put a checkmark in the appropriate box. If the question cannot be answered affirmatively, leave the box blank.

The purpose of this exercise is not to defend the content of your beliefs. The purpose is rather to see where you are in your values system and what needs to be done if you are to make your stand on any given issue a real value. The inventory helps you find out how you arrived at your convictions and how firm you are in them.

Questions on Value Processes

1. Was my decision made *freely* without external force or coercion?
2. Do I *cherish* the position that I have taken?
3. Did I do my homework, that is, did I carefully evaluate the advantages and disadvantages of my decision and thoughtfully consider the *consequences?*
4. Did I make my decision after examining all possible *options?*
5. Have I practically *applied* and *acted* on my convictions and beliefs?
6. Have I given *public affirmation* to what I believe?
7. Does my behavior indicate that I act on these beliefs *repeatedly* and does it reveal a definite pattern and personal commitment?*

SESSION 6

Leader's goal: to discover more about the participants' personal goals.

Participants' goal: to identify personal goals and compare them with the biblical imperatives already identified.

Key exercise:

Ask each person to jot down eight personal goals for the next ten years. You need not be concerned about getting them listed in any proper form or sequence—simply jot down your hopes for yourself for the medium-term future.

Distribute to each participant the following list of personal needs. Try to coordinate each listed goal with one of the five categories of personal needs. For example, if a person had listed as a goal "getting a better paying job," that person would score one point under "Security" because the goal in question has primarily to do with personal maintenance and survival. Continue to relate the goals to personal needs—scoring one point for each goal that most closely coordinates with a listed need.

Add up the points under each needs category in order to get a profile of the person's real needs. Notice what the stated goals reflect about that person's current needs and interests.

Personal Needs

Security: Primarily concerned with maintenance, survival, keeping life on an even keel.

Affiliation: Concerned about relationships, being close, having personal friendships.

Power: Concerned about recognition, having impact on others, being in charge, leading, managing.

Achievement: Being successful in accomplishing a specific task.

Self-fulfillment: Doing something that is intrinsically interesting and productive for you.

Ask the participants to compare their stated goals and the needs these tend to meet with the biblical imperatives discussed in Sessions 1 and 2.

At the conclusion of these six sessions the pastor should have a good deal of information that can be of help in determining which persons might fit well with others in an action group— persons who are feeling a pinch, want to do more, or are already engaged in pastoral care ministries. Obviously, it is important to provide more than just one such study session in order to encounter a sufficiently large number of people from which to make a selection. In our experience, work with at least forty people is usually advised before any attempt is made to identify those who might be ready for further participation in an action group.

Recruiting Members

Each candidate for a caring ministry should be contacted individually. Share with them why you think they might find participation in such a group meaningful. Buttress your conclusions with things you have heard them say in the past and with what you have heard about them from others. If they respond in a way that confirms your perception of their readiness, suggest the possibility of their joining with others in a common endeavor. It will probably not be possible to specify at this point exactly what the proposed group will actually be doing, but it is surely possible even now to make an initial "contract" with the person as to (1) who else is invited; (2) how many times the group will meet before deciding whether to continue; (3) how long the meetings will last; (4) when the meetings will be held; (5) what you yourself will do; and (6) that if the group decides to continue, it could be either a support group or an action group.

Getting Acquainted

From six to twenty people should be an adequate number for the first meeting. Fewer than six is too few. More than twenty may inhibit sharing or introduce such a wide diversity of interests as to overwhelm the members. New people can be added at subsequent meetings, but more than twenty at any given time could prove cumbersome and difficult to manage.

We recommend that at the first meeting you reiterate the "contracting" information you shared with each person individually. This will clarify any misunderstandings and help transform the commitment from an individual contract—made only between you and each person—to a group contract binding everyone present.

Making a collage can be a helpful exercise for getting persons better acquainted with one another. The theme of the collage should be whatever specific issue brought the group together. Materials could be on hand in advance: picture magazines with plenty of color photos; sheets of newsprint at least 2' x 3' in size, scissors, and scotch tape or glue.

Ask the participants to pick out from one or more of the journals those pictures, words, or other symbols that can suggest or communicate their feelings about the theme that brought them together here. Have them arrange the cutouts and affix them to the newsprint. Allow them half an hour to make their collage.

Then have each of them share their experience with the whole group by holding up the collage where everyone can see it, telling what it means, and asking for questions or comments. Allow at least ten minutes per person for this sharing of the collages.

To vary the exercise one might ask the participants to make a nonrepresentational drawing that depicts their present situation or to draw a time line of their life history (either their whole life or perhaps just the past year or three years). This kind of sharing helps people experience themselves and others and gives them a feeling that they are sharing important information. It moves the group from fear toward trust.

Another useful device involves the paraphrasing of Bible passages. Choose passages which have some obvious relevance to the group and its central concern. Distribute a different Bible passage to each individual. Then ask each person to write the passage in his or her own language and in terms of today's world. For example, Ezek. 34:27–29 reads as follows:

> They shall know that I am the Lord when I break the bars of their yokes and rescue them from those who have enslaved them. . . . I will give prosperity to their plantations; they shall never again be victims of famine in the land nor any longer bear the taunts of nations.

A member may paraphrase it thus:

> The Cambodian people will know that God is the Lord when they are rescued from the atrocities that are confronting them. They will have plenty to eat, they will have land and a home, they will have good jobs, their children will be educated, and their families will be reunited.

When the people have completed their paraphrase, suggest that they write the outline of a story or event which, if it took place today, would be like the one in the Bible passage. For example, the paraphrase just cited might lead to a story such as this:

> The Lim family fled from their home in Cambodia because they were persecuted by the government and by their neighbors. After risking their lives in a crowded boat on the open sea they went to a relocation camp for three months. They prayed daily that they would be rescued from the torments of overcrowding, scarcity of food, and lack of privacy. One day they were told that a church in Michigan offered to pay to bring them to its community where they would be loaned a house, helped to find a job, taught to speak English, and given enough food and money to live on until they were established. They were thankful to God for their new opportunities.

After ten minutes for developing their outline ask the members individually to share their story and discuss it. This exercise too is helpful in getting people better acquainted, and in leading them to both reflect on the biblical imperatives and dialogue with the biblical meanings.

Setting Goals

Determining the direction and style of a group requires that its members individually become clear about their own personal goals, particularly as these relate to the rest of the group. It is important to look not only for common denominators that might facilitate group development, but also at "where the people are actually coming from," so that group life and group goals can be displayed in ways that will also help individuals to meet their own personal goals.

Identifying Personal Goals

After two meetings devoted to helping members get better acquainted, the group should be ready to begin identifying personal goals. A goal is that which a person or group intends to do, including an indication not only of the activity but also of its result. Goals can be formulated at many levels: they can be very broad (scarcely to be achieved in this lifetime) or they can be quite specific (measurably concrete and achievable by a certain date). We differentiate between these two categories by referring to the former (more general) as goals and to the latter (more specific) as objectives.

Certain criteria are operative in the selection of effective personal goals. Members may be reminded that goals (1) include an indication of both the activity and the result to be accomplished by it; (2) are important to me; (3) relate to my skills and to any other purposes I may have; (4) are something I want to accomplish; and (5) are believable within my frame of reference.

"Eliminating white racism," for example, does not meet these criteria. It is hardly believable that one person could achieve such a goal, nor does the formulation in those terms give any clues as to how to accomplish it. Specificity about results as well as activities helps to produce a goal which is more attractive because more achievable: "Through affirmative action planning, talking with people in my office, training, and reading, I will seek to racially integrate my office." That is an attractive achievable goal; it articulates what needs to be done and specifies the context in which it will be done. True, what for one person is "too vague" may for another be "too specific," but the point here is simply to find directions or tendencies that can be helpful in planning, not to bind oneself to hard and fast rules.

While easy to identify, goals may be difficult to select. To list possible goals is not difficult. In fact, many people are constantly thinking up new things to do. They have lots of ideas about how to eliminate sexism, clean up the environment, and provide economic or legal justice for poor people; they may also have many personal goals for getting their children through college, taking next year's vacation, advancing a career, finding an enjoyable hobby, and removing excess weight around the waistline. Everyone is constantly finding and identifying goals. The problem is how to choose one or more to act on.

To help the participants find and choose goals, ask them to read certain indicated passages from the Bible that have relevance to holistic, action-oriented pastoral care. Divide the membership into smaller groups of two or three, and ask these small groups to make a fanciful drawing of the meaning of their particular passage that they can share with the others. This process, like the one described earlier, helps people both to remember the biblical passages and to explore their relevance. After the small groups have shared their drawings, all participants should make a list of the various goals that might have been arrived at by the people who either wrote or were depicted in the several biblical passages. Save these lists for the next meeting.

At this next meeting (the fourth) remind the participants of the goals that surfaced at the previous session. Ask them to choose amongst these goals in order to find and identify their own personal vision of what they want for themselves. Now is the time to have people dream about the future and try to envision what it would be like if their own best hopes were to be realized: for a perfect day, a perfect week, their ideal home (or city or church) ten years from now. Tell them to sit comfortably and just let their imagination roam. Fantasize about the future. Picture this fantasized world. Describe it in detail. Allow about ten minutes for this exercise. Then have the members write down the results of their experience and, afterward, share them with the group.

Once these fantasies have been shared, ask each individual to make a list of their personal goals for achieving that future. Include no more than six or eight such goals. These lists are not to be shared at this time. Direct the people instead to take their list home and talk about it with others they trust outside as well as inside the group. Ask them as they talk, to think about these ideas. Tell them to eliminate from their list any goals that seem gradually to be losing their value or attraction. At the next meeting each member should bring only those two or three goals that still seem most important personally and most relevant to what this group might become and do. These remaining goals can be discussed at the fifth session.

Group Goals and a Common Pinch

If the group is made up of people you thought might be experiencing a common pinch—that is, experiencing similar difficulties with such common problems as aging, or a defective school system, or anxieties about transportation—this common concern should have emerged in the process of formulating personal goals. At the point where the personal goals are shared, it is important to look for this common denominator.

If the goals articulated do not reflect this common concern, ask the group whether such concern does in fact exist. If it does, and the people had simply not written it down, ask them now to write personal goals that could describe what they might hope would happen with respect to this concern.

If the reported goals do show a commonality, try to help the group identify it and become more specific as to how they will address it. A process for helping clarify how the group will address its concern will be discussed in the following chapter.

Group Goals and Engagement-Reflection

If the people you are working with do not feel a common pinch, if their desire to do more grows rather out of simple gratitude for what they have already received, then moving toward the discovery of a common interest will be a more complicated process. It will probably require an intermediate step that we call engagement-reflection.

Engagement-reflection is a process whereby people are brought out into the larger community to help them find and experience potential areas for a caring ministry. We assume that there is in every person a need to help others, but we also realize that for most of us there is very little interest in looking for trouble. It is much easier and safer *not* to go out into strange situations, with strange people, seeking opportunities for ministry. The feelings experienced are much like those that discomfort us when we join a new congregation. We feel awkward trying to find ways to communicate with strangers in a strange environment. These same feelings occur as group members go out into the world looking for needs and for opportunities to serve God's people.

Some members will resist, saying that only one or two persons are really needed to gather the data for the group: it duplicates effort if everyone goes, and besides it makes decisions more difficult when people come back with a lot of different ideas. Other members may express approval of the idea outwardly, but there will be no congruence between what they say and how they in fact behave.

We once asked members to go to a seamy downtown area and observe the life there on skid row, talk with the people who frequent the place, eat with them, and experience whatever was there to be experienced from 10:00 A.M. until 2:00 P.M. One of the men in our group willingly complied. He took three others with him to a very fancy restaurant that happened to be in that same blighted area. He and his party spent almost their entire time in that delightful restaurant. They had seemed to go along with the idea, but didn't really "get into it."

Engagement-reflection takes people not only out of their accustomed neighborhood but also out of their habitual patterns for gathering information and processing it, understanding it, and making decisions based on it. In social action, church people tend to operate more from their thinking, logical selves than from their sensate, feeling, intuitive selves. This is why experiencing the world in a new way will give them not only new information but also a new sense of anxiety and threat with respect to the realities experienced.

The process of engagement-reflection is built around the idea that people must experience in order to understand. It assumes that people must continually be in dialogue with the community if they are to respond and react responsibly. Consciousness is indeed shaped, if not actually created by the media which bring it information. In order to increase sensitivity, develop full and deep understanding of the world's needs, and have the greatest possibility of responding appropriately, a person needs not secondhand information but direct experience. This is why the engagement-reflection process requires members to go beyond their familiar newspapers, television programs, and magazines and get out into the world to experience what is happening.

Procedurally, the group is divided into small teams of two or three persons each. Before the group starts to do its problem defining, goal setting, and action planning, these small teams are sent out into the community during a period of no more than three months (preferably three to four times a month) to experience what is in fact happening out there in the community. Their experience is not haphazard but structured, with advance discussion and determination of places to go, what to look for, ways to observe, what to bring back, and how to assure careful listening, feedback, support, and sympathy.

Before people are sent out into the community it is wise to make some initial decisions with respect to the areas of concern with which the group might be working. Choices about where to begin gathering information obviously will strongly affect the determination of the kinds of issues likely to emerge as arenas for pastoral care. In choosing these initial arenas we have found it effective to use a method developed with John Biersdorf at the Institute for Advanced Pastoral Studies.

Before the group meets, buy copies of the latest edition of the daily paper read by most of the people. Have at least one complete edition for every two people present.

Ask the participants to go through the paper and clip segments that mention or allude to issues of interest. (These can be issues discovered in perusing the newspaper or issues that emerged from previous discussions.) Ask participants to note down in writing the two or three issues that seem most important to them and about which they would like to know more.

Some members may want to explore only one issue. Others, however, may be interested in two issues, and still others in three or even more. Once the participants have a list of the issues in which they might be personally interested, a "force-field analysis" is used to make priority choices: For each issue of interest ask people to list that issue at the top of a separate sheet of paper and draw a vertical line down the center of the sheet. At the top left side, underneath the name of the issue, write Forces Attracting Me. On the right side, underneath the name of the issue, write Forces Repelling Me. Then participants are asked, in a time of quiet and reflection, to think of the forces that either attract or repel them with respect to working on that specific issue. They should be encouraged to be alert for anything that comes to mind: the importance of the issue, their past experience with it, their own personal fears in getting involved in that area, the feeling that they are already too busy to do anything. Whatever comes to mind that actually affects a person's information or motivation with respect to working on that issue, and seems to be significant as either an attracting or a repelling force, should be noted. Participants are to draw a line and on it list a *name* for each such force. The *length* of the line should be roughly proportionate to the intensity or power of that particular force.

After the participants have done this force-field analysis for each of the issues of interest to them, they are to rank the issues in priority according to their own personal interest in working on such issues. These rankings can then be used as a basis for dividing the members into small teams to work on one or more of the specific issues.

While the participants are doing their force-field analysis, get out eight sheets of newsprint, and at the top of seven of these sheets write the name of one category of social issues, a category likely to hold greatest interest for the largest number of participants (in the past we have listed these seven: women's issues, jobs, hunger, health care, aging, energy, and racial issues). On the eighth sheet, write "other issues." Hang these eight sheets in various parts of the room.

When all the people have finished their force-field analysis, ask them to choose one issue on which they would like to work for the next month. Have them walk to that area of the room where the newsprint hangs which identifies the general category of their preferred issue. If they do not see their issue listed on any sheet, they should go to the sheet marked "other issues." People sharing similar interests have now been grouped into task forces organized around the various social issues.

As people come together in these several areas of the room ask them individually to explain their interest to others there in the same location and see if a common concern is discernible. If only one or two people are present at any location, ask them either to join another group or try to convince persons at another location to join them at theirs. Each team should have no fewer than three members.

Once the teams are formed, it will be important to determine the kind of engagement-reflection experience each will have. This determination should *not* be made at the meeting at which the teams are formed. Planning should await the next meeting, at which the teams will choose how and where they will go to be involved in the engagement-reflection experience.

Three kinds of engagement-reflection experiences are worth considering: the issue exposure, the unstructured exposure, and the case exposure. We have found it best to use only one of these and not try to do all three. It is possible, of course, to mix a part of one with a part of another, but we recommend against trying to do all these with the same group.

The Issue Exposure

The purpose of the issue exposure is to explore only one issue, such as racism or criminal rehabilitation. Everyone involved in this planned engagement-reflection experience is given an assignment. Everyone is also given training in observing and asking questions. On one occasion our issue exposure centered on air pollution. The planners of the event identified several "springboards" from which the team of participants was to "plunge." Some team members were sent to interview environmental planners, others went to government regulatory agencies, and still others to firms and organizations suspected of being major producers of the pollution. Some team members talked with people who were particularly victimized by the conditions—homeowners in areas of high smog density, farmers whose crops were deteriorating or even destroyed as a result of atmospheric blight, and persons who lived a short distance downwind from the huge refuse-burning city dumps. From these first contacts, the "plungers" discovered other places they could go and persons they could talk to in order to learn more about the causes and effects of air pollution.

Initial research is a key to this kind of experience. In issue exposure the issue is determined either by the participants themselves or by the group leaders. People come together at least twice a month to report on their experiences and interviews and to find out how things are going. In some groups these feedback sessions occur weekly. At such group meetings each team is asked to share their learnings in whatever way they think best. Sometimes full reporting requires two or three evenings. It is important that ample time be allowed for in-depth exploration of every person's experience.

The Unstructured Exposure

We use the unstructured exposure in instances where no common interest has emerged on which a particular group might wish to work. One kind of unstructured plunge is that used at the Urban Training Center in Chicago. There each participant was asked to wear the worst possible old work clothes, leave all money behind, and spend three to five days on Skid Row. The "plungers" must find ways of surviving: they must seek shelter, food, money, jobs, handouts, or whatever they can find to maintain their existence. This kind of engagement-reflection experience puts the participants in touch with the existent economic, justice, and helping systems of the community. It also demonstrates the trials of people who personally are without resources.

Participants return to tell of their journeys: the dragons met, the jungles and sloughs encountered, the fair maidens lost (and in some cases found), and the triumph of the pilgrimage survived. From these stories the group can more specifically identify issues and gather data of value in the process of choosing a workable problem.

For people unable to invest three to five days in such an experience we often use another type of unstructured exposure. In this engagement-reflection experience we assign people to certain "beats" over the course of a month. Some will be asked to "hang out" around the pizza parlor, others to talk with as many people as possible in a certain neighborhood, others to go to the schools (with the permission of the administration), others to the prisons (the chaplain is often an excellent entry point), and others to city council meetings. Sometimes the group agrees that all the "beats" should be within a certain radius of the church building, or within the area defined as the parish. People are sent to these "beats" without an agenda; they are told to listen, to watch, to participate, and to feel what is happening to them and about them.

The Case Exposure

In the case exposure participants are asked to focus on a particular event rather than on a piece of geography or a specific social issue. Like the issue exposure, the case exposure requires preplanning. In one such engagement-reflection experience we had a seminary class look into all the ramifications of an alleged incident of police brutality. We divided the participants into discrete investigating teams for separate visits to the police, the city council, the community from which the alleged victim had come, and citizens groups organized to defend the alleged victim. Other teams were sent to the university to talk with experts on the sociological and psychological causes and effects of such incidents. Yet another team interviewed pastors in the area.

It was not necessary to tell these seminarians what they ought to believe about the case. With a vast amount of nearly firsthand information, they came to a deeper understanding of all the forces at work in the situation: the sociological forces, the impact of the various government agencies, the influence of black pride, and the relationship of the church to the event.

Following the experience not everyone, of course, arrived at the same conclusions. There was, however, greater agreement among the participants than had been apparent before the engagement-reflection. Thus, it was possible to involve a substantial part of the group in action projects related to the incident because (1) they understood the issues; (2) they knew from face-to-face conversations the people involved; and (3) they cared about what happened to these people.

As the participants in this case exposure came to know and understand the people directly affected by the police policies and practices, they were less confused by what seemed at first to be impossible and impenetrable structures and systems. As through firsthand experience they came to know and care about the people, they were motivated to do something. Their face-to-face conversations with governmental and business leaders showed these persons to be less formidable and powerful than was formerly assumed. Thus, the anxiety once generated by ignorance of "what is out there," by feeling that events are out of control, was reduced. People who participate first by listening and then by acting feel less victimized by the systems at work in the world.

Once the teams have completed their particular engagement-reflection experiences, it will be necessary for the whole group to become more specific about its area of main concern. This is accomplished by allowing team members to report on the contacts they have been making and to share what they have been learning. Some of the teams may be less effective than others. Maybe their members will not do the work, or will not have much to contribute. These people should be encouraged to join other groups where they might have a better experience in learning about the needs of the community. If it turns out that more than one group is doing well and getting increasingly interested in what is happening in the community, it may be necessary to develop more than one action group. In other words, a group should be encouraged to divide if differing commitments begin to emerge. Following such a division, the members of each new group should be asked to invite others who might want to work on the issues being explored.

A number of procedures are thus involved in getting an action group started. One must first find out who might be interested in participating. Then it is necessary to hold initial "team building" sessions. Information must next be gathered—either from the people in the group or from the community through engagement-reflection experiences—in order to determine specific areas of concern in which the group wishes to be involved. Goals need to be identified and specifically chosen. Only then can one get on with the process of involving the group concretely in meaningful action.

4. Developing an Action Plan

When the members of an action group have coalesced around a common interest, either on the basis of a mutual problem (a common pinch) or as the result of an exposure experience (wanting to do more), they come to the point of asking the question: "Shall we continue as a group?" If the answer is yes, they will want to face the further question: "Will ours be a support group or an action group?"

A support group serves a variety of functions all at the same time. It is at once a staging area, a training center, a hospital, and a retreat, all taken together. While engaging in various caring-action ministries, the members also come together at least once every two weeks to help each other with the following tasks: (1) identify personal goals for ministry; (2) identify ways to implement the goals; (3) share plans and actions with the group; and (4) pray, reflect, celebrate, analyze, and evaluate together.

Our use of the word *ministry* here is not accidental. Participants in a support group are involved in one form of being the church. They increase the dedication of their ministry as together they share their problems and concerns, clarify their intentions, and advise on planning and implementation. Because such support is ministry, we recommend that the group recognize members by commissioning them in the name of Christ to carry out their specific goals.

The support group can continue for as long as it proves helpful. New members can be added along the way. Those who are added, however, should be guided through processes of goal finding and goal choosing such as the rest of the group experienced earlier.

As the support group continues to meet regularly, its members listening to one another's struggles, it serves several functions. Members provide psychological support to one another in their particular situation. If a member brings a particular problem, the group may brainstorm alternative actions, suggesting places where further help might be found and exploring the ramifications of each alternative. Individuals working on a particular problem may at times wish to "contract" with other members for specific help or assistance.

The support group can also function as an accountability resource. When a member says, "I am going to confront my boss about this problem," or "I am going to write my representative in Congress," it is appropriate and expected that at the next meeting someone will ask, "What happened when you confronted your boss?" or "What did you say in your letter to your legislator?" Questions such as these call the participants to account and remind them of the tasks they have chosen. We shall have more to say about the organization and functioning of a support group in the next chapter. It is one option for groups that decide to continue.

The other option for people who have coalesced around a common concern is an action group. The action group focuses on one specific goal toward which all the members direct their energies corporately. In the beginning, of course, its purpose need not be very specific. In its early stages the group will be looking for some kind of commonality among its various members. If the participants decide they want to go on and continue working with each other, and if they discover similar directions in which they want to go, they then have the possibility, through more data gathering, to identify specific change targets.

The question of continuing is of course answered in the very choice to become either a support group or an action group. However, it can also be answered another way: The members may agree, "We've had an interesting time together and good conversation, but continuing the group does not seem right at this time." That too is a valid decision. It is important for a group to know not only when to start but also when to quit. Allowing the group to disband is as creative as seeing it go on. It is not a sign of defeat.

If the group decides to continue, certain attendant behaviors and attitudes can support your confidence in that decision. You may wish to watch for whether (1) most members come to most of the meetings; (2) enthusiasm for staying together is clearly articulated; (3) empathy and concern for one another are openly expressed; (4) members involve themselves in helping one another even outside the group; (5) members talk with each other between group sessions; (6) conflicts or differences between the members are expressed within the meetings rather than outside; and (7) mutual enthusiasm prevails for being involved in a particular area of ministry.

It is not necessary that all these criteria be met before continuation can confidently proceed. A group may decide to continue, for example, even though some members are not enthusiastic about doing so! However, where the aforementioned criteria—including enthusiasm—are largely lacking, any plan to go on should proceed with caution—as an experiment for a specified period of time.

How does a group decide either to disband or to move toward becoming an action or support group? We have found the following procedure helpful at this stage. Each participant shares with the group two or three personal goals. After these goals are written on a chalkboard the members are asked to identify any common themes that seem to be emerging among them. Once the common themes have been identified, the group should discuss whether the goals listed seem to suggest important reasons for staying together. After feelings about continuing the meetings have been aired, the group must decide whether in fact to continue. Do not vote on this question! In a matter of this kind the majority does *not* rule. Simply ask the group if they would like to keep working together. If there is no objection, proceed to deciding whether to be an action group or a support group. If there is objection, explore what the consequences might be should one or two or even more members choose not to participate in subsequent meetings. If you do not have enough people (at least six) committed to continuing, then disband. It is better to disband the group than try to find sufficient numbers of "replacements," for the new recruits would not have the group's background of experience in goal finding and goal choosing.

Formulating Goals and Objectives

If the group decides that continued existence for the sake of corporate action is appropriate, it will need to establish group goals. This can be done by reviewing the goals of the individual members and by recalling the common themes and priorities discovered in prior discussions. A small subcommittee of one or two persons can be asked to write a tentative draft of the group's goals between meetings. These goals will probably need to be refined and modified later. For the time being, however, this first draft can provide the working goals that will give the group identity and direction.

Workable Problems

With an understanding of the biblical vision, a deepening awareness of the members' personal visions, and a firsthand experience of community needs, the group can begin to choose its focus for ministry. This will not be easy: there are so many things that need doing; there will be conflicting interests and ideas expressed; and many tasks that could be tackled will seem beyond the resources of the group.

The group will need to sort out the various possibilities and focus on workable action plans. We have found the following process helpful in determining the problems that are indeed workable.

Start by recognizing that there is no "root cause" or absolute beginning to any problem. Do not try to "get to the bottom" of something before attempting to change a situation. That is neither necessary nor possible. To assume that there is only one cause of a problem is to place the blame on one particular group—and social problems are seldom perpetrated by only one group. Further, the "one cause" assumption can result in an endless search which only delays attempts to effect change.

Black poverty in the United States is a cogent example. It has many causes: segregated housing, inferior ghetto school systems, job discrimination, poor transportation to places of work, and white racism. All of these causes are real; none is primary, none secondary. If one is interested in doing something about black poverty, one must begin where the resources and interest are, not where the "root cause" may lie. If education is of interest to the group, work at that. To wait until all the causes of all racial problems have been ferreted out could mean a long wait.

The common pinch discovered earlier or the group's exposure experiences will have disclosed problems upon which the group might initially work. It is important to formulate and list these problems in such a way as to enhance understanding and commitment, and thereby to lessen confusion while heightening communication. Problems all too often are stated in such a vague way that they only confuse people and heighten anxiety. A few years ago white suburbanites were paralyzed when told that the root cause of black poverty was their white racism. The defensive responses were immediate: "In what respect? What makes you think I am a white racist? Wherein has my attitude been wrong? How have I behaved badly? Do you think I was ever a member of the Klan or the Nazi party?" Only after such questions were pursued at considerable length did people gradually begin to understand the depth and reality of the problem. Clear definitions help communication and keep the attention directed toward the quest for understanding and answers. To arrive at such clarity we like to think in terms of what we call workable problems.

Defining the Problem

A workable problem is defined in a certain way. To formulate the problem it is necessary to clarify who is doing or not doing what. The definition names the actors and describes which of their activities need to be changed. A workable problem needs to be seen and defined in the light of certain characteristic criteria:

1. It is specific. It points to something that people can see, feel, hear, taste, measure. To the degree that it is vague, it will only increase conflict and controversy. Since there may well be enough controversy anyway, such controversy ought to focus on

the intrinsic issues rather than on a misunderstanding about the formulation of the problem.

2. It describes a behavior or policy about which one can do something. This criterion cannot always be met, but the group should at least move in the direction of choosing such social change targets as admit of a real possibility of success. Some people of course need to make a witness against social ills about which very little can or is likely to be done in their lifetime. But Christians who invest their time and energies in social change should devote the bulk of their effort to areas where there is the greatest possibility of meaningful change.

3. It is not pejorative or a deliberate putdown. "Throw that stupid mayor out of office" may be a specific enough target, but it is unlikely to generate clear and open communication among all the affected parties, nor does it clarify what the mayor did that was wrong. To help determine whether the problem definition is on target we often ask: "Are people on all sides of the issue likely to agree with our definition of the problem?" All sides may not agree on the need for change, or on our set of priorities, but, as far as possible, our statement of the problem should be acceptable to all—formulated to describe what is actually happening rather than to incite conflict.

4. It is not something from the past but something that is now going on or is about to occur. Definitions that describe what has already happened are not productive. They focus on what cannot be reversed. That may seem obvious, but groups are often frustrated where this point is forgotten.

The Merger Process

Sometimes, after having been through the exposure-reflection process for several meetings, the group will quickly and easily arrive at clarity about what needs to be done and what it wishes to do. The members will see a need and pinpoint ways to meet it —without going through much of a process to help them identify and formulate their workable problems. If, however, the group does *not* arrive at this kind of clarity—as happens about half the time—we have found it helpful to introduce the "merger process" to facilitate their efforts.

On 3″ x 5″ cards participants write out from two to five problems that they think the group should address. (For the sake of
assuring more careful and extended individual thought on the
matter it is sometimes helpful to give this task as a homework
assignment rather than simply asking for spur-of-the-moment
ideas immediately after raising the subject.) The people then sit
in pairs, each person sharing his or her problem with a partner.
Each one explains to the other why these particular problems
were chosen. If the two persons have problem statements that are
almost the same, merge the two lists. If some of the problems
listed are different or contradictory, write them out on a fresh
list formulated *by the pair.* As the two talk about their problem
statements, some of the formulations may sound inappropriate;
these should be dropped.

Once all parties have shared their lists in pairs, each pair finds
another duo and the sharing is repeated in groups of four: one
new statement is made for any two problems that are alike, and
those problems that cannot be mixed (merged) are listed separately—or dropped if the original author wishes. Then merge
again by having groups of four get together with other foursomes
and do the same thing. After merging these lists, ask that all
merged lists be put on newsprint to be hung on the wall and
read aloud.

Now comes the task of choosing a statement for the entire
group. If possible—and especially if feelings are running high
and there is a lot of disagreement—wait until the next meeting
before attempting to reach a decision. This allows time, not for
the conflict to go away, but for people to make the best possible
case for what they feel is important. While waiting, individuals
will be talking to one another on the phone, gathering more
information, and doing whatever they can to help shape the group
decision. Everyone will receive as much information as possible
in advance, and the decision itself, made at the next meeting,
can perhaps be by consensus.

Setting Objectives

Once the group has adopted as its own one or more workable
problems, it should reassess its goals. Are the goals previously set

(at the time of deciding to continue as a support or an action group) still valid? If so, proceed to the task of setting objectives. If not, redo the goals and then set the objectives.

Once the goals are agreed on, the group needs to decide how they are to be achieved. That is, the group needs to formulate objectives and project a work plan. An objective, as we have seen, is a more specific form of intention than a goal. A well-written objective (1) identifies a measurable result, (2) names the action to be taken to accomplish it, (3) sets a date by when it will be completed, (4) says who will do it, and (5) relates to the goal.

With regard to measuring the results of an action, it should be noted that results that are measurable only by counting (dollars, heads, or number of times an activity is performed) can often be uninteresting, superficial, and peripheral to what a church or action group exists to do. If you set out to raise $1,000 or increase attendance by 10 percent you have an objective that is measurable all right, but one that does not mention the reason for the action. A more provocative objective indicates in quantifiable fashion *why* raising the budget or the attendance is important. The following contrasting statements may help to illustrate alternative ways of conceiving and formulating objectives:

Through five calls per week, the pastor will bring the Christian message of hope to people who are shut in, grieving, or hospitalized. (*Not:* the pastor will make five calls per week.)

The committee will determine through dialogue and testing the sales practice or "open housing" policy of the real estate office. (*Not:* the committee will have dialogue with the real estate office as to its policies concerning open housing.)

The social action group will determine its goals this quarter. (*Not:* the social action group will hold six meetings this quarter.)

Objectives should not be difficult to agree upon in an action group. Once the workable problems have been defined by the group as a whole, subgroups can generate a list of specific objectives. Then the membership as a whole can usually arrive at a consensus about which of the several objectives will receive group implementation.

Objective-choosing can be made even easier through a process of brainstorming the criteria for selecting such objectives. A half-dozen criteria have proved particularly helpful to us in considering each objective. The objective will be (1) within the group's financial and time resources, (2) related to group members' skills and abilities, (3) within the group's usual norms (an abortion clinic for a Catholic church would ordinarily not be appropriate), (4) important, (5) interesting to the group, and (6) something the group wants to do.

Implementing a Work Plan

Once the objectives have been selected, it is important to identify all the activities or jobs that must be done to accomplish the task. Jim Anderson, staff member of the Episcopal Diocese of Washington, has suggested an excellent device for doing this. Have the members write on 3″ x 5″ cards all the activities that need to be performed, using one card for each activity. These cards are then taped onto a wall or chalkboard one at a time, each located according to the sequence in which the numbered activity needs to happen in relation to its predecessors—first, second, third. As the cards are moved about, the "flow" begins to emerge until finally agreement is reached with respect to the proper sequence of all activities required.

Then the group will need to agree on: (1) who should do each task—their names are written on the appropriate card, and (2) when the task should be completed—the appropriate date is also written on each card. Someone can then record the whole action plan for the entire group.

With written objectives in logical order, the group is ready to write a work plan and implement it. Evaluation should routinely accompany all the work as you go along. These steps involving implementation are the most exciting—and the most threatening! When the going gets rough, there will be the temptation to stop the action and start the planning all over again. If the need to go back to "square one" seems to be based primarily on fear, resist it. Of course, you will want to revise and redo as you go along in the normal course of events. But don't get caught in the planning-forever-in-order-to-avoid-movement syndrome.

As you develop and implement your work plan, keep in mind

John Westerhoff's sensible guidelines for responsible use of power:

1. Avoid blaming the victims—it is not the fault of the poor that they are poor. Correspondingly, always see yourself as part of the problem; never permit a "we the liberator" vs. "they the oppressed" attitude to develop.

2. Permanent change is slow and gradual. While never as fast as it morally ought to be, social change may tend to reverse itself unless it proceeds slowly enough to gain acceptance. Where significant systemic change is envisioned think in terms of five years, not one month. Be patient, but never lose a sense of urgency—the two go together.

3. Don't fall in love with your solutions. Even the best laid plans of mice and men often come to naught. Creative ideas can lead to negative consequences. Maintain a sense of humor. Don't take yourself too seriously. Be willing to compromise.

4. Strive to see every problem through the eyes of the oppressed, repressed, suppressed persons. Let them become involved in envisioning and acting for their own good. Your responsibility is not to do things *for* them—that would be patronizing and oppressive; you are rather to join *with* them to create an alternative future.

5. Don't be as concerned to eliminate an evil as to create a good. Be aware of people's hurts but respond with vision.

6. It is terribly time-consuming to be repeatedly starting new groups for working on social problems. Use existing communities and organizations where you can. Always involve as many people as possible.

7. Think innovation. A small acceptable addition to existing ways will gradually cause significant change in the present system.

8. Love your enemies. Never use violence. Have faith that you are not alone. Remember that goals and means both need to be justified.

9. Periodically withdraw from the action to seek new perspective. Retreat to pray. Act and reflect; reflect and act. Celebrate your little advances and even your reversals.

10. And, most important, struggle daily with the Word of God as well as the problems of society. Live each day with your newspaper in one hand and the Bible in the other. Let the Scriptures judge and inspire your plans and actions. Take up your cross, but do all for the glory of God.*

Getting an action group started is not easy. We have touched briefly here on the various steps involved: identifying potential group members, recruiting the members, contracting with them, getting acquainted, building a team of people that trust one another, identifying the personal goals of the members, and choosing to continue as an action group or support group. If the group chooses to be an action group, it then identifies potential areas for involvement, chooses an area of involvement, gathers information, sets goals, identifies workable problems, writes out its objectives, formulates a work plan, implements the plan, and evaluates its work as it goes along.

The important thing is that you take your time and move deliberately and faithfully. For most clergy and laity impatience causes the greatest difficulty. Leaders sometimes expect the group to move easily, quickly, and gracefully. That rarely happens. Effective and loving leadership helps people express and face their own resistance and provides the tools to keep moving ahead.

5. Working with People Already in Action Ministries

Besides the people feeling a common pinch and the people who want to do more there are likely to be—as we mentioned earlier —a number of people in your congregation who are already involved in various action ministries. Your approach to social action would hardly be complete without them. It is important to know who they are and what they are doing. You may discover these people through a campaign of home visitation or through the study groups mentioned in chapter 2. A questionnaire can also be useful in this connection.

Christ Church (Episcopal) in Grosse Pointe, Michigan, developed a helpful instrument of this sort for their purposes. Their Outreach Committee sponsored "A Celebration of Outreach," beginning with a simple letter commending members for their financial and service-action involvements beyond as well as within the walls of their own parish and inviting members to list these various involvements in an anonymous questionnaire. The results were to be tabulated to afford a profile of the congregation's ministry of outreach, and eventually be celebrated at an appropriate point in their public worship. The multi-page questionnaire by its columns and captions helped people think of their involvements as either local or national; as either church-related, agency oriented, or personal in the sense of not being connected with any organized group; and as falling generally into such categories of concern as education, the judicial and penal system, politics, quality of community life, the arts, public health, fund raising, and "other." In addition to suggesting all these diverse areas and levels and kinds of support and service, the questionnaire also provided within its many sizable blank spaces (awaiting individual entries) brief illustrative involvements ranging from Sunday School librarian to volunteer tutoring at school, from canvassing for the March of Dimes to letter-writing for Common Cause and contributing to the Detroit Symphony.

On the basis of information gathered by these various means the church could act in a number of ways with respect to these active people. It could (1) organize support groups, (2) organize action groups, (3) provide skill training workshops, (4) revamp an existing social action committee, and (5) provide public recognition of present involvements.

Support Groups

Support groups have already been described in chapter 4. We mention them again here with special reference to people who have already had a history of involvement in social action. A support group made up of such individuals could enter into a variety of activities: working for international peace, feeding the hungry, improving the school board, developing ministries for the aging. It could aim primarily at being supportive to people who are generally involved in the same social change issues, for example, members of the same profession who might be interested in exploring the relevance of the gospel to, say, teaching, medicine, or law. It could offer a forum for those who have a common interest and actively participate in social concerns and who would welcome the chance for discussion without developing new plans for broadened activity.

Such support groups are obviously more feasible in large congregations or in interchurch or interdenominational settings where significant numbers of people may participate. A city-wide peace group in Los Angeles served just such a function. It brought together people from a variety of different peace action ministries, elicited information about other peace activities, provided a clearing house for the various activities, gave a forum to those who wished to recruit for a particular "event" or campaign participants from outside their own group, and offered support to workers when they were away from the pressures of the immediate action.

Support group activity of this sort can allow you to utilize fully and deeply your pastoral care skills and at the same time to contribute to healthy social action. Especially important in this setting is the opportunity to help people explore their feelings. Some of these feelings may have been generated in earlier life situations. Other feelings may be based on what the activists are now experiencing. Through careful listening and accurate feedback you can help these people sort out their feelings as you provide a profound caring ministry to hurting people engaged in social action.*

Ministry to persons in social action is often very difficult. Some of them are self-righteous and have contempt for feelings and interpersonal relationships. In many instances, however, much of this bravado is a facade, an attention-getting device used much as a child seeks attention from a parent by showing off or acting naughty. Patience and continued caring will be required of you in such cases as these social activists test you to see if you truly believe they are lovable. Often their "hard nosed" style is a defense they adopt in order to protect themselves against future loss. They fear that the caring relationships developed in the course of an action might be too precious to give up if their loss were threatened. Such loss would be too painful to bear.

In addition to reaching out in love to group members who may make that task difficult, you can also develop exercises to help such people actually support one another. Contentious people seek attention in the best way they know. Though their method of asking may be inappropriate, that for which they hunger can still be provided. And if it is, this can have profound impact on their future behavior.

A social action support group can also be helped to reflect on other needs in the world beyond those presently engaging their efforts. They can also be helped to deepen their integration of the Bible and their daily involvements. Gordon Cosby, at the Church of the Savior in Washington, D.C., has written a *Handbook for Mission Groups*† which may be helpful in this connection. The mission groups he describes stand midway between an action group and a support group as we have defined them. Cosby offers useful suggestions for opening the participants of a support group to a deeper awareness of their spiritual journey as well as their social action journey.

Action Groups

In addition to support groups, action groups can also be created for people who have already been involved in caring ministries. For this to happen two factors are necessary. First, the potential members will have to be recruited "between" social action projects. Most active persons do not need yet another project competing for their time and energies. Each person has to set work limits. Nonetheless, in the case of people who are already at work, you should be alert to the possibility of involving them the moment they begin to disengage.

Second, the potential members will need to have some prospect of reconciling and uniting conceivably diverse interests with a view toward a common goal. People who have been involved in social action over the years are usually fairly clear about what they think is important. It will be necessary therefore to select people who are likely to find common interests within the framework of their established commitments and concerns.

An action group can easily get so focused on the action that the members pay little or no attention to the group processes, to interpersonal relationships and the inner life. Indeed such failure can often lead to the demise of the group. There may well be some initial resistance to dealing with these personal and interpersonal concerns. Expecting such resistance and planning in advance on how you are going to deal with it can help you minister to these people. We recommend that with experienced action people you start slowly in addressing these concerns, but regularly keep inserting experiences which will help the people face and deal with them.

Skill Training Workshops

People already active in social ministry can be helped to become more skillful and effective in their particular action project. To move in this direction, you might begin by identifying the skill training needs of your group. This can be done through face-to-face interviews, though after you have come to some tentative conclusions about needed training it would be well to check out your perceptions with the group.

We have found that denominational staff and staff people from ecumenically supported projects are excellent resource persons for doing training with social action groups. Their costs are usually covered by the denomination. Generally they have been chosen for their job because of their experience in the field. They have already had some successes in training and are oriented toward the practicalities of organizing and implementing social change ministries. Nonetheless, check first with several people you know well to find out if the person you are thinking of asking is indeed the right person. State specifically for the trainer you invite the outcomes you hope for, including the kind of training processes expected. Some available people are better at lecturing than at facilitating experience-based learning.

For persons already involved in social action we have found it helpful to provide various kinds of training workshops: recruiting and organizing an action group; analyzing social issues; analyzing government power structures; setting action goals; managing conflict; briefing on a specific social issue; and reflecting on the biblical and theological aspects of a specific social issue.

Social Action Committees

Too often people elected or appointed to social action committees are chosen in order to fill organizational vacancies on such committees rather than to provide specific ministries. As we have seen, such people may not have the skill, the predisposition, or the personal needs to do an effective job. Social action committees are commonly composed of well-intentioned individuals who have had little or no experience in concrete action. They are hardly ideal for either a support group or an action group.

Some social action committees of course are not designed for action. They only fund projects. Deciding on the use of church funds for worthy projects, however, can be done without going through the processes described in this book. Such a group can simply study the various proposals available in the light of its particular priorities and concerns.

If the social action committee is to be either an action group or a support group, members should be recruited because they have something to contribute or because they think the group will help them fulfill some of their personal goals. The committee should of course be accountable to the church's governing body by way of regular reporting and review.

It is a common problem for the social action committee to get bogged down in attempting to address too many current and important issues. Often the committee is unable to function effectively because it has not narrowed its focus. Dealing with this problem successfully may mean giving up a number of crucial issues, even those in which some committee members may have invested much time and effort. The conflict that thereby ensues will be real. But the resulting focus of energy can mean an increased probability of successful action, in which case the short-term pain will be offset by the long-term gain.

Recognition

As leader of a voluntary organization, you are doubtless already aware of how important public support and recognition can be to the nurture of members. Many needs of the workers themselves can be directly met by some kind of public recognition. Such recognition can be accorded in a variety of ways:

Organize a social action festival where all the people involved in corporate or individual projects can share their efforts and learnings. This could be a pot-luck supper, a congregational meeting, or an all-day Saturday event.

Invite specific persons involved in social action to plan and conduct a series of worship services, perhaps over the period of a year, to highlight their biblical visions, personal visions, and perceptions of a needy world. These people could either preach the sermons or work with the pastor in developing the pastor's sermons for such a series.

Invite specific persons to write a column in the church newsletter reporting on their activity or the activities of others.

Organize an opportunity for the social action people to serve on regional and national denominational committees addressing similar issues.

Bring in national and regional staff persons to speak to a committee and to the whole church about the denomination's work in a particular area. The social action persons could take active leadership roles in relation to these events.

The focus in all these endeavors is on recognizing what is already being done in social action ministries and supporting and celebrating the accomplishments and efforts of the people who are doing it. Even where a church is itself doing little in the way of organized, institutional social action, many Christians in the congregation may well be committed to important ministries. Applaud the action that is there and find ways to strengthen and support it.

6. Overcoming Blocks to Action

The process of helping people take greater responsibility for themselves, their church, and their work often generates resistance. The sources of such resistance need to be identified and exposed. In many instances pastoral care skills can then be effectively employed in dealing with them.

It may be useful here to take a closer look at a number of these blocks to action as they are encountered in social action ministries. We will examine the following: fear of social action and conflict, competing values, fear of failure and scale paralysis, lack of skill, peer pressure, lack of reward, inappropriate motives, inappropriate social goals, and ineffective methodologies.

Fear of Social Action and Conflict

Many individuals within the church fear social action. They try to steer clear of it themselves and keep it out of their congregations as well. This fact has been borne out in recent decades by the institutional losses incurred as a result of social action activities in the churches. The United Presbyterian Church in the USA, for example, experienced substantial losses in membership and income when people learned that a group connected with the denomination was providing financial aid for the legal defense of radical black activist Angela Davis.

Most churches also fear conflict. Like other institutions in the society, churches too disagree as to the nature of our social problems and what should be done about them. Traditionally such disagreement has been politically institutionalized in the political parties. The party system gives legitimacy to divergent views and philosophies. Local congregations, however, rarely have comparable mechanisms for giving organizational or institutional legitimacy to divergent viewpoints within their constituency. Churches often place primary emphasis on "unity in Christ." They strive for harmony at all times. Church people are embarrassed by differences in their midst, whether in matters of doctrine, liturgy, or even politics. Such differences can often divide denominations and congregations, or groups within them. Moreover, nonideological factors such as location or accessibility are also operative in producing homogeneous congregations. It is hardly surprising therefore that in such a context the churches, being institutionally precarious voluntary organizations, should shun conflict and seek to avoid social action issues on which there may be little consensus.

Churches act more eagerly on issues about which there is considerable agreement, such as food for the hungry abroad. On issues involving disagreement, in such areas as education, medical care, sexism, or size of the military budget, the church finds action difficult.

Added to these organizational difficulties is the tendency of many churches to focus on personal and private sin and salvation as over against corporate sin or responsibility. This individualistic emphasis is theologically not consistent with the words of the judges, kings, prophets, and poets of the Old Testament, or of Jesus. But many Christians simply lack the theological and historical sense or experience to perceive God's call for national repentance or to understand what is meant by corporate salvation.

Believers who hold that God calls both individuals and communities to repentance cannot deny the very real difficulties that confront the church in this connection. It is not a matter simply of our having too many timid clergy or lay leaders who are excessively cautious about social action programs in the congregation. There is more to it than that. Sometimes the very thrust of our theology also resists.

It is all the more important, therefore, to recognize the churches' fears and to design and implement strategies that will make the social action efforts even more effective in achieving their goals and in attracting further support from the institutional church. Indeed we ourselves, in our programs and training, are committed to this approach. Pastors or action groups who do not look realistically at the congregation's social norms are likely to frighten, alienate, and confuse people. That is both unhelpful and unnecessary. We favor those social action processes that are institutionally effective. Such processes affirm and support all the people. They address empathetically the fears of those who resist and they build on small successes.

A prudent approach of this sort requires that people be helped to identify and share their fears. Some people have probably had negative experiences with social change in the past. Not talking out the fears related to those experiences can actually heighten apprehension concerning change. This is especially true if church leaders are themselves enslaved by the same fears. Sharing fears can of itself often help to alleviate them. Simple sharing, however, is not effective if the listeners' fears are compounded by the anxiety of others, especially the leaders in the group.

We have found the following process helpful when there is anxiety in a group. Everyone is asked to sit quietly for about five minutes and make two lists, one titled: "If everything goes wrong in this situation, what are the worst things that could happen?" and the other: "If everything goes right, what are the best things that can happen?" The people then come together in small groups to share their lists, and a representative sample of hopes and fears from each small group is finally shared with the entire membership. The leader's acceptance of each expression of personal concern, the leader's calm ability to allow others openly to express themselves will often be enough to take the debilitating edge off the fears. At the same time the hopes articulated during the process can also reinforce each person's drive for growth.

Some members may have a fear of what could happen within the group. It may be helpful to discuss such fears openly. For example, a person may say, "I am afraid that people will leave here in a huff before the meeting is over." The group can face this possibility and discuss what to do about it. Perhaps the members can agree in advance on a specific time for adjournment, the hour when everyone will leave the meeting. Exceptions can of course be made in advance for people who at the beginning of the meeting announce their early departure time. Members might also wish to talk about appropriate and inappropriate expressions of anger; classification of that distinction could help them feel more in control and less manipulated by their emotions.

Where there is an abundance of fear or anger and conflict, the group may wish to devote an entire meeting just to training in the development of skills for dealing with it.* Such a training event can begin to change the group's expectations about anger and conflict. It can increase each participant's skill in managing conflict, and add to each person's tolerance for dissension.

Competing Values

Competing values can also block social action. When individuals or groups differ on the importance of certain issues, action often cannot be taken until a consensus is reached. And that may take a long time. Sometimes people never can choose one course over another. Their ability to act is blocked because they are genuinely caught between two competing values, values that have equal attraction for the group or in some cases seem equally repulsive.

John, a lay leader, strongly values success in his chosen profession; he wants to earn a substantial salary and be perceived as highly competent. At the same time, he wants a full and deep life with his family and church. Succeeding at work takes nearly all his attention and energies, yet he still wishes to devote substantial amounts of time to family and church. The two values compete. Because John does not feel confident about where to place his priorities, his action is at best erratic.

A social action group may well find itself caught up in such a value competition. The members may be almost equally concerned for race relations, ecology, care for the elderly, and the economy. All these concerns will weigh so heavily upon them that the group will not know which issue to address. One contemplated action may block another. For example, their concern for world hunger and poverty may motivate them to want to act to provide free or low-cost grain to starving people abroad, but their concern about the price of bread for poor people here at home may prevent such action.

It is a help to people confronted with competing values if they can be enabled first of all to identify what those values are and then how they are in competition. As values are clarified, many conflicts and disagreements will diminish or disappear. Writing or speaking of specific values can often help to eliminate false conceptions. The group may even find that the conflict no longer exists.

We have found a pair of exercises helpful in such situations. We use them in sequence. First, have the participants list ten items that describe "Who I am." These ten attributes or characteristics may be either negative or positive. The list might include such items as: white, male, teacher, self-confident, plays the guitar at parties, short-tempered. It is perfectly all right if some of the items seem to be contradictory. Once the list is complete, the participants are asked to choose that single attribute which is most characteristic of themselves, that is, the one without which they would be somebody else. After this is done by each participant, the list is shared openly with the group. It is helpful to inquire as to which attributes are contradictory, which seem to be in conflict with one another. For example, is "short-tempered" contradictory to "self-confident"? Which seemingly negative attributes may in fact be strengths? How? Which strengths may interfere with other strengths? The exercise will normally take about two or three hours, usually a whole meeting, for a group of ten.

Then at the next meeting, ask the participants to do the exercise described for the fifth study session in chapter 3 above. Both these exercises are as useful to individuals as to groups. Individuals often see their highest priorities, and the group finds commonly held values and areas of possible agreement.

It may be that, even after clarifying values and determining priorities, the group still experiences conflict. Improved communication is in itself no guarantee of unanimity. Sometimes it only clarifies more fully the real disparity of values. If so, this may be the time to stop looking for agreement, especially if there are no other values and goals to bind the group together. This may be the point at which to ask the question: "Based on our understanding of our disagreements, can continuation of the group serve any purpose?"

If the group nonetheless finds reason to continue, there are two other options: divide into two groups with different purposes, or vote to determine a single direction. If a vote is taken and the majority is not overwhelming (more than one-third opposed), the potential of a group commitment to action is obviously not high. However, the vote is nonetheless determinative: those who stay in the group can now proceed to action rather than delay any further.

Fear of Failure and Scale Paralysis

Quite apart from the fear of social action and the fear of conflict is the fear of failure, the uncertainty about success. Unless people sense that their action is going to be productive, there is likely to be a normal and healthy resistance to getting involved. Most people will quickly lose interest. They would rather invest their time and effort in a situation where success is a probability. Why spend yourself where failure seems assured? Why give such activity any priority at all?

We use the term "scale paralysis" to refer to the resistance experienced when an action is felt to be puny compared to the magnitude of the problem. Scale paralysis is the result when I feel I have only a slingshot with which to fight a giant. It derives from the gap between the scale of our resources and the scale of the problem. Scale paralysis often tells us something worth hearing—and dealing with. Theologically, the point is that we are not called upon to resolve all human misery, but only to respond in faith with what resources we have.

There are three methods to combat fear of failure and scale paralysis. The first is obvious—start small. Build on successes as you develop your group and your action plans. In tackling small problems and achieving your goals in relation to them, you are less likely to be significantly concerned about lack of future successes. By choosing manageable targets you can practically eliminate the problem of being paralyzed by fear of failure.

Second, join with others. Many effective and important social action movements depend on participation by people other than those who initiated them. Your group does not have to be the first to think up a project, or the sole controlling agent in its implementation. Explore existing programs in your community that might benefit from your support. The scale of resources will be perceptibly multipled.

Third, continually and emphatically underscore the importance of the small steps your group is accomplishing in relation to the larger issues of the society. Taking meals to twenty shut-ins does not eradicate poverty, but it is a measurable contribution to the massive needs of the poor. Protesting the misuse of $1,000 in school board funds for personal travel does not eliminate graft from government bureaucracies, but it does keep public officials on notice that their actions are being carefully monitored.

Lack of Skill

Another block to action is the members' sheer inability to function well in expected ways. Often the people simply lack the basic skills that are obviously required—and all too often taken for granted.

We once led a group project in which the assignment was to interview various members of a city council. The group members were given a month to make specific appointments, hold the specified interviews, and report back. When the group assembled at the end of the month, not one person had done any interviewing. Why not? The members did not know how to make an appointment. They didn't know what to say in order to get an interview. They didn't know how to deal with it when they were being "stalled." They were also uncertain about just what they wanted to learn. In short, the people had been asked to carry out specific tasks before they had even learned how to function in ways appropriate to the job.

We subsequently provided these people with training in interviewing and in making and carrying out appointments with city council members. We not only showed them certain techniques, but we also had them practice. One would take the role of a council member, another the role of the interviewer. They practiced in the presence of others and received feedback on what they did well and what they did poorly. The purpose of the interview as well as its processes were clarified at the same time. Through practice people gained the confidence that they could do the job. The following month the results were much better.

The best skill training is practice. Talking about what might happen is helpful. Demonstrations are useful. But there is no substitute for directly involving people in the actual work they are to perform. We have usually found that it is not possible to do "on the job training" with our groups. It is not possible to go to an actual interview with the participant, observe what was said and done, and then give feedback to the interviewer. Because this is not possible, we have found role play* and simulation† very helpful. Through such devices, the participants try out new behavior, get support and criticism, and actually improve their needed skills.

Peer Pressure

Peer pressure is another potentially important block to action. Nobody likes to face situations that might jeopardize personal relationships. Liberals, for example, might be afraid to complain about high taxes lest their friends begin to think they are back-tracking on their traditional support of aid for economically de-prived persons. This fear of one's peers is related to an individual's own sense of self-worth. If I place great weight on my being acceptable to others, then I will probably move cautiously so as not to jeopardize valued relationships.

People engaged in social action sometimes experience uncertainties about how their friends and peers may regard them. The fears are dealt with in part by the growth of a new sense of belonging in relation to the group itself. As a new "in-group" develops, it becomes a reference point to which the individual can turn for support and affirmation, thus counteracting fears that may be generated by peers outside the group. The sharing of personal concerns, hopes, fears, and vulnerability among group members helps to develop between them the trust that all of us need.

In addition to leaning on the support group for strength, the individual should be helped to an increased acceptance of self and a diminished reliance on the approval of others. One way to do this is to identify each individual's present strengths. David Johnson in his book *Reaching Out* offers an exercise that can be helpful in enhancing regard for the self:

1. Think of all the things you do well, all the things you are proud of having done, all the things for which you feel a sense of accomplishment. List all your positive accomplishments, your successes of the past. Be specific.

2. Divide the group into pairs and share your past accomplishments with one other person. Then, with the help of your partner, examine your past successes to identify the strengths you utilized in achieving them.

3. Share with the whole group the full list of your strengths. Then ask the group, "What additional strengths do you see in my life?" The group then adds to your list other qualities, skills, or characteristics that you have overlooked or undervalued. The group feedback should be specific; if members tell me that I have a particular strength, they must back up their feedback with concrete evidence of a behavior that demonstrates that strength.

4. After all group members have shared their strengths and received feedback on what further strengths others see in their life, each member should then ask the group, "What might be keeping me from utilizing all my strengths?" The group then explores the ways in which you can free yourself from factors which limit the utilization of your strengths.

5. Think about your past successes and your strengths. Think about how your strengths may be utilized to improve the number or quality of your close relationships. Then set a goal for the week ahead concerning how you may improve either the number or the quality of your close relationships. Plan how the utilization of your strengths will help you accomplish this goal.*

Lack of Reward

Workers on the social action team will be more committed and competent if in their own lives they can see some real rewards of the effort. The greater people's personal reward the greater the involvement. Where the process of changing racist patterns of behavior can bring personal benefit, white people are more likely to change their behavior. As long as the maintenance of established racist patterns works to their advantage, they will do little to change them. If business people can see that the provision of equal employment opportunity for all races strengthens their business and the country, they will be more likely to support equal employment opportunity.

We have provided training experiences for persons whose purpose was to help church people seriously explore and deal with their white racism. Feeling it was important for people working on racism to be aware of their own self-interest in eliminating racist practices, we had the participants build a list of the reasons the group wanted racism eliminated. Their group effort generated a significant list of reasons why it is to each white person's advantage to help change current practices. Some blocks to action can thus be removed by helping people see the rewards that are likely to attend involvement in such actions.

Inappropriate Motives

At the beginning of a social action group particularly, inappropriate motives often surface as a source of resistance. Social action programs occasionally attract persons who have strong personal needs that can be detrimental to effective program development and are not likely to be met through the work of the group. Some people, for example, are angry at all forms of authority and are just looking for opportunities to act out that anger; these persons come to the social action process in quest of something to be against. Others operate out of closed ideological systems; their personal rigidity makes group flexibility over the course of the action very difficult.

Both of these types should be dissuaded from participation in the social action group. The people who come to social action motivated chiefly by anger will neither help the group nor be helped by it. Those who use rigid formulas may be operating out of a great deal of fear, and while their rigidity may help them to deal with an overwhelmingly frightening world, it too will neither help nor be helped by the group. People marked by such excessive anger or rigidity need to be counseled by persons who are competent to deal with these issues in a setting other than a social action program. We recommend that you refer such people to a therapist or invite them into an ongoing counseling relationship with you.

Inappropriate Social Goals

We always start our work with a clear and open understanding that certain goals are out of bounds for a Christian group. The church's social mission is grounded in a biblical vision of the Kingdom of God. All the action programs that a church group undertakes must be evaluated in terms of this vision. Goals, for example, that seek to continue racist or sexist policies or practices are clearly inappropriate, just as people who seek to dehumanize, humiliate, or take away dignity from persons, or destroy the environment in such a way as to make the globe less habitable, are hardly appropriate members of a Christian action group.

At one of the first sessions of any group you may want to have the members make a list of goals that would be deemed inappropriate for this particular group. Such an exercise will help allay fears among the members that some activities ahead may conflict with their faith and conscience. Being specific about what is *not* to be done will also increase trust.

We did this with one group that was particularly leery about what we "social action types" might do. Working together, the group made a list of the things in which we would definitely not get involved. This list included such things as "Trying to change the government by illegal means," "Supporting programs to use the military to overthrow a legitimate government," and "Supporting a particular candidate for political office." It went on to include other agreed-upon items: "Using secondary boycotts to pressure business," "Demonstrating and picketing to change hiring practices," and "Making drug laws more lenient."

Some people's fears about "goals" reflected more a concern about the methods to be used than about the actual ends to be achieved. Some items on the list mentioned goals that we as leaders might personally have supported. In agreeing to what was on the list, however, we were contracting with the group that we would not lead them in directions which they felt were inappropriate. We felt it important to start where we could. The procedure and the contract helped the members feel that they had some control over what was to happen and that they would not be led toward something that they did not want.

During the discussion process that produced the agreed list, we were able to point out personal disagreement with several items suggested for inclusion. Some of these items the group— or the individual making the suggestion—subsequently removed on their own initiative. Other such items were retained; despite our contrary views on the matter, the group simply felt strongly that these should not be changed. So we agreed together that these would not be pursued as group goals. Dealing openly with people's fears about goals they deem to be inappropriate can often remove certain blocks to action.

Ineffective Methodologies

A variety of social action methods have proved to be less than effective. These too can constitute a block to action.

Studying the problem for too long a time can pose such an impediment. Many times groups think it necessary to wait until they have all the data before they try to move ahead. Unfortunately, they will *never* have *all* the data. There will never be a time when all the information is finally in hand and nothing is any longer ambiguous. There must be a time, therefore, when a group will simply use what they have, inadequate as it may be, and move ahead.

Another methodological question has to do with the multiplicity of issues addressed. Sometimes a group will attempt to address so many issues that there never emerges a sufficient focus to allow for the development of concrete action strategies. We recommend that the group keep its efforts sharply focused.

Finally, the habit of always opposing and never proposing can stymie action and make it ineffective. Simply to be against something is too limiting. If you want to involve others, especially people who understand power, you must focus on and develop plans that actually propose something, seeking to create an arrangement better than that which now exists.

Conclusion

We have indicated ways of identifying potential recruits for the various kinds of social action groups one is likely to organize in a local congregation. We have tried to suggest ways of putting such groups together, and procedures for matching the personal needs of its members with the purposes of the group. We have even proposed approaches for dealing with common blocks to action.

The rest of the job is now up to you. Take your time. Start small. Don't expect to be able to tackle large projects immediately. If you are optimistic, persistent, and organized, your chances of success will be greatly increased.

The fear of social action is probably the single most important factor inhibiting ministries in this arena. From our own research we know that most failures in ministry do not come from choosing to be involved in social action; they come from lack of interest in program development on the part of the pastor, from incompatible leadership styles, or from personality clashes between the pastor and the people.* Other research has shown that involvement in social action has no effect whatever on a congregation's growth or decline in membership; in other words, participation in social action is not something that hurts the church institutionally.†

With the material here at hand to guide you, with your knowledge that social action does not necessarily lead to destructive conflict, and with your faith in God's support and presence, you should now be able enthusiastically to develop both thrusts of holistic pastoral care—counseling *and* action. With each supporting the other, a full, meaningful, and rich ministry can be developed.

Notes

Page
2. *Carl Rogers, *Client-Centered Therapy* (Boston: Houghton Mifflin Co., 1951); Seward Hiltner, *Pastoral Counseling* (Nashville, Tenn.: Abingdon Press, 1948); David Roberts, *Psychotherapy and a Christian View of Man* (New York: Scribners, 1951); Wayne Oates, *Introduction to Pastoral Care* (Nashville, Tenn.: Broadman Press, 1959); Carroll Wise, *Pastoral Counseling, Its Theory and Practice* (New York: Harper, 1951).
3. *Saul Alinsky, *Rules for Radicals* (New York: Random House, 1971); Gibson Winter, *The New Creation as Metropolis* (New York: Macmillan, 1963); Harvey Cox, *The Secular City* (New York: Macmillan, 1965); George Younger, *The Church and Urban Renewal* (Philadelphia: Lippincott, 1965); George Webber, *The Congregation in Mission* (Nashville, Tenn.: Abingdon Press, 1964); Colin Williams, *What in the World* (New York: Office of Publication and Distribution, National Council of Churches, 1964); Thomas Wieser, *Planning for Mission* (New York: U.S. Conference for the World Council of Churches, 1966).
6. *Edwin Schur, *The Awareness Trap: Self-Absorption instead of Social Change* (New York: McGraw-Hill, 1976).
7. *Dennis T. Jaffee, "A Counseling Institution in an Oppressive Environment," *Journal of Humanistic Psychology*, 13, (Fall 1973): 25–26.
7. †Abraham Maslow, *Motivation and Personality* (New York: Harper & Row, 1954).
7. ‡James MacGregor Burns, *Leadership* (New York: Harper & Row, 1978), p. 117. Burns's italics.
7. §These findings are mentioned in Len Sperry, Douglas Mickelson, and Phillip Hunsaker, *You Can Make It Happen* (Reading: Addison Wesley, 1977), p. 71.
8. *Victor Frankl, *Man's Search for Meaning* (New York: Simon & Schuster, Pocket Books, 1963), p. 158.
8. †Karl Menninger, *Whatever Became of Sin* (New York: Hawthorn Books, 1973).
9. *E. Clinton Gardner, *Biblical Faith and Social Ethics* (New York: Harper & Row, 1960), p. 187.
10. *Howard Clinebell and Harvey Seifert, *Personal Growth and Social Change* (Philadelphia: Westminster, 1969).
10. †Douglas Lewis, ed., *Explorations in Ministry* (New York: International Documentation on the Contemporary Church, 1971), p. 5.
10. ‡Daniel Day Williams, "Theological Reflections on the New Modes of Pastoral Care" in *Explorations in Ministry*, pp. 240–56.
11. *Ibid., p. 242.
11. †For further information about these projects write to the Institute for Advanced Pastoral Studies, Box 809, Bloomfield Hills, MI 48013; Well-Spring, 11301 Neelsville Church Road, Germantown, MD 20767; and Eagles, Inc., P.O. Box 67, Dayton, OH 45405.
12. *Don Browning, *The Moral Context of Pastoral Care* (Philadelphia: Westminster Press, 1976)

Page

12. †William Clebsch and Charles Jaekle, *Pastoral Care in Historical Perspective* (New York: Prentice-Hall, 1964), pp. 8–9.

15. *Daniel Day Williams, *The Minister and the Care of Souls* (New York: Harper Brothers, 1961), p. 37.

17. *Other helpful resources are: Howard Clinebell, *Basic Types of Pastoral Counseling* (Nashville, Tenn.: Abingdon Press, 1974); David Switzer, *The Minister as Crisis Counselor* (Nashville, Tenn.: Abingdon Press, 1974); and Harvey Ruben, *Crisis Intervention* (New York: Popular Library, 1976).

18. *William Ryan, *Blaming the Victim* (New York: Pantheon, 1971), p. 240.

19. *Studs Terkel, *Working* (New York: Pantheon, 1974), pp. 292–93.

21. *Pam Conrod, *Newsweek*, 13 August 1979, p. 15.

24. *See, for example, Robert K. Hudnet, *Arousing the Sleeping Giant* (New York: Harper & Row, 1973) and Gibson Winter, *The Suburban Captivity of the Churches* (New York: Macmillan, 1962).

25. *Alfred Plummer, *The Gospel According to St. Luke* (New York: Scribners, 1910), p. 368.

30. *See, for example, the Office of Church Life and Leadership, *Church Planning* (New York: The United Church of Christ, 1976); John Westerhoff, *Tomorrow's Church* (Waco, Tex.: Word, 1976); Jim Fenhagen, *Mutual Ministry* (New York: Seabury Press, 1977); Gordon Cosby, *A Handbook for Mission Groups* (Waco, Texas: Word, 1975); Barbara Kuhn, *The Whole Lay Ministry Catalog* (New York: Seabury Press, 1979).

30. †Westerhoff, *Tomorrow's Church*, pp. 113–14.

31. *Office of Church Life and Leadership, *Church Planning*, pp. B:3–7, 8.

32. *This exercise was written by John Biersdorf for a curriculum of the Institute for Advanced Pastoral Studies called "The Whole Church Project Leader's Manual."

36. *Sidney Simon, *Meeting Yourself Halfway* (Niles, Ill.: Argus Communications, 1974) pp. 36–37.

59. *Westerhoff, *Tomorrow's Church*, pp. 95–96.

63. *See Reuel Howe, *The Miracle of Dialogue* (New York: Seabury Press, 1969) and Virginia Satir, *Peoplemaking* (Palo Alto, Calif.: Science and Behavior Books, 1972). Both of these books were written for other audiences and concerns, but their insights are easily translated into useful resources in the realm of social action ministry.

63. †Gordon Cosby, *Handbook for Mission Groups* (Waco, Tex.: Word, 1975).

70. *See Speed Leas and Paul Kittlaus, *Church Fights* (Philadelphia: Westminster Press, 1973); James Allen Sparks, *Pot Shots at the Preacher* (Nashville, Tenn.: Abingdon Press, 1977); Robert Alberti and Michael Emmons, *Your Perfect Right* (San Louis Obispo, Calif.: Impact Pubs., Inc., 1970), and Sharon Bower and Gordon Bower, *Asserting Yourself* (Reading: Addison Wesley, 1976).

74. *See Norman Maier, Allen Salem, and Ayeaha Maier, *The Role-Play Technique* (La Jolla, Calif.: University Associates, 1975) for a discussion of role-play procedures and twenty role-play situations.

74. †In the appendix of Leas and Kittlaus, *Church Fights*, there is an extended discussion of how one particular social action simulation, "The Cities Game," can be used as a learning technique. The most complete guide to simulation resources is David W. Zuckerman and Robert E. Horn, *The Guide to Simulations: Games for Education and Training*, (Lexington, Mass.: Information Resource, Inc., 1973). Available from Information Resource Inc., Box 417, Lexington, MA 02173.

75. *David Johnson, *Reaching Out* (Englewood Cliffs, N.J.: Prentice-Hall, 1972), pp. 145–48.

79. *See unpublished research done by the Alban Institute on the Involuntary Termination of Pastors.

79. †See General Assembly Mission Council Minutes of the Presbyterian Church in the USA, 1976, pp. 336–97.

Annotated Bibliography

Anderson, James, and Jones, Ezra Earl. *The Management of Ministry*. New York: Harper & Row, 1978. An excellent book on the nature and purpose of ministry; includes both practical and theoretical material.

Biersdorf, John. *Creating an Intentional Ministry*. Nashville, Tenn.: Abingdon Press, 1976. A helpful collection of articles on negotiation, planning, career assessment, and social action.

Browning, Don. *The Moral Context of Pastoral Care*. Philadelphia: Westminster Press, 1976. An important theory piece on pastoral care.

Dittes, James E. *The Church In the Way*. New York: Scribner's, 1967. A valuable introduction to psychological theory and its relevance to the local pastor's work.

Hessel, Dieter. *A Social Action Primer*. Philadelphia: Westminster Press, 1972. An introduction to social action theory and theology, with a helpful taxonomy of social action methods for the church.

Hoffman, John. *Ethical Confrontation in Counseling*. Chicago: University of Chicago Press, 1979. A discussion of the relationship between ethics and therapy.

Hudnut, Robert. *Arousing the Sleeping Giant*. New York: Harper & Row, 1973. A practical guide to introducing social action and planning to a whole congregation.

Johnson, David W. *Reaching Out: Interpersonal Effectiveness and Social Action*. Englewood Cliffs, N.J.: Prentice-Hall, 1972. A compendium of training exercises.

Leas, Speed, and Kittlaus, Paul. *Church Fights*. Philadelphia: Westminster Press, 1973. An introduction to intergroup conflict in churches.

Lewis, Douglas, ed., *Explorations In Ministry*. IDOC, 1971. A compendium of reports from experiments in bringing together counseling and social change.

Menninger, Karl. *Whatever Became Of Sin?* New York: Hawthorn, 1973. A readable, interesting call for clergy and behavioral scientists to "cry comfort, cry repentance, cry hope" in order to both heal and prevent social and individual trouble.

Napier, Nina, and O'Neill, George. *Shifting Gears*. New York: Avon, 1972. This helpful little book has many practical ideas on helping individuals deal with change in their lives. It can be used by an individual or by a leader who is looking for exercises with a group.

Phelps, Stanlee, and Austin, Nancy. *The Assertive Woman*. San Luis Obispo, Calif.: Impact Pubs., Inc., 1975. An introduction to assertiveness training with exercises and practical ideas for enhancing assertiveness.

Schur, Edwin. *The Awareness Trap*. New York: McGraw-Hill, 1976. An oversimplified but provocative critique of the personal growth movement.

Seifert, Harvey. *New Power For the Church*. Philadelphia: Westminster Press, 1976. Relates concerns for social action with concerns for congregational health and growth.

———. *Power Where the Action Is*. Philadelphia: Westminster Press, 1968. An introduction to a variety of social action approaches for the Christian.

Seifert, Harvey, and Clinebell, Howard. *Personal Growth and Social Change*. Philadelphia: Westminster Press, 1969. A good introduction to pastoral care and social action; with helpful theory and lots of good ideas about what to do with groups.

Research and Development Division of the National Council of the Young Men's Christian Association. *Training Volunteer*

Leaders. YMCA, 291 Broadway, New York, New York 10007, 1974. A compendium of training exercises.

Westerhoff, John. *Tomorrow's Church*. Waco, Tex.: Word, 1976. A biblical and theological apology for getting involved in social action, and a step-by-step plan for getting church people into social action.

Williams, Daniel Day. *The Minister and the Care of Souls*. New York: Harper & Row, 1961. This classic on the theology of pastoral care is still in print and of real use to both preacher and counselor.

Wise, Carroll. *Pastoral Counseling, Its Theory and Practice*. New York: Harper & Row, 1951. An introduction to pastoral care.

DATE